SCRAPS
Organized
~ to ~
Perfection

DeLoa Jones

American Quilter's Society

P. O. Box 3290 • Paducah, KY 42002-3290

www.AQSquilt.com

Located in Paducah, Kentucky, the American Quilter's Society (AQS) is dedicated to promoting the accomplishments of today's quilters. Through its publications and events, AQS strives to honor today's quiltmakers and their work and to inspire future creativity and innovation in quiltmaking.

Editor: Jane Townswick
Graphic Design: Lisa M. Clark
Cover Design: Michael Buckingham
Photography: Quilt photos by Charles R. Lynch
            Quilts in settings and how-to photos by David L. Jones

Library of Congress Cataloging-in-Publication Data
Jones, DeLoa
  Scraps : organized to perfection / by DeLoa Jones.
    p. cm.
    ISBN 1-57432-791-7
  1. Patchwork. 2. Quilting. I. Title.
    TT835 .J65 2002
     746.46--dc21

                                        2002002721

Additional copies of this book may be ordered from the American Quilter's Society, PO Box 3290, Paducah, KY 42002-3290, or online at www.AQSquilt.com.

CONTENTS

As an avid quilter for more than 20 years, I have always found it hard to part with any piece of fabric, no matter what its size or type. Even the tiniest scraps call out to me, telling me that they could become part of a pieced or appliquéd flower that needs just their colors.

Each time I make a new quilt, I get caught up in the creative process and excited about the design unfolding in front of me. In the creative throes of making a current masterpiece, I simply cannot bring myself to stop and throw away leftover fabrics. That's why, after moving to a new house two years ago, I found myself surrounded by ten boxes that were all labeled with the same words "Miscellaneous Fabric." As I began unpacking those boxes, I realized that they might easily contain anything from 1" cut strips to pieces as large as a yard or more. In a way, the boxes were like money in the bank – a significant resource of treasures that I could use to great advantage in my quilts. I continued unpacking my stash of scraps with energy – the sooner I had them organized, the sooner I would be able to start making all the beautiful quilt designs that were floating around in my mind!

Scrap quilts have always been a love of mine, filled with memories of past projects and the people I made them for. To me, scrap quilts are like beds of flowers, with each piece of fabric working together to create a spectacular display of color. I like the way that the colors in a scrap quilt make my eyes dance across the surface, noticing different fabrics each time I look at it. Even the fabrics I like to call "uglies" have their place in a scrap quilt. They can act as a visual resting place or create a bridge between colors that are more exciting. I like to call these things "happy accidents" – things that can only happen in a scrap quilt, where chance allows you to produce color combinations that are both beautiful and unexpected.

Scraps have other benefits as well. You can use them to experiment with colors and find out if a block design will work the way you hope, before going to a store to purchase fabric for a whole quilt. Along with quilt books and your own creative ideas, your scraps can become a valuable resource in your quiltmaking. Try to keep your stash of scraps within easy reach wherever you work on your quilts. When they are at your fingertips, they offer an immediate source of creative solutions to many different kinds of quiltmaking concerns, and they often inspire unanticipated ideas for new designs.

In the following pages, you will find my techniques and hints for organizing and using scraps effectively and a selection of wallhangings and larger quilts that are made from scraps. Wall quilts are given in one size, and for larger quilts, you will find Size charts, Fabrics and Supplies charts, and Cutting charts that list all the information you need for making that quilt in a range of sizes from baby or lap quilts to full, queen or king-size.

I hope you will enjoy adapting my way of organizing scraps to your unique sewing area and that making scrap quilts becomes a regular part of your quiltmaking life. With each new project, your scraps will increase and multiply, until you have enough for the next lovely design that tugs at your heart and mind. Enjoy putting together some exciting scrap quilts that will become your own unique family heirlooms.

DeLoa Jones

CHAPTER 1: GETTING ORGANIZED

Organizing your scraps into groups of same-size pieces and shapes will enable you to easily take advantage of this great fabric resource. My organizing system involves cutting scrap fabrics into strips and other commonly used shapes, like squares and triangles, and storing them in individual bins, where they are quickly accessible. The following processes work well for me, and you can adapt them to your own quiltmaking needs. The first step is to make sure that you have a sharp or new blade in your rotary cutter, for cutting accuracy.

AUTUMN GLORY 84½" x 107½"

Machine pieced and quilted by DeLoa Jones

I changed the value in half of the outer blocks, which produced a different look in the border of the quilt. It was a happy accident that occurred because I ran out of one type of fabric and substituted another.

STRIPS

Start by deciding what widths of scrap strips you would like to store. Think about the kinds of quilt patterns you like to make most often. Initially, I cut my scrap fabrics into 1", 1½", 2", and 2½"-wide strips, and then decided to add 1¾"-wide strips, as well, because that particular width was so great for making Log Cabin quilts. Organize your scrap strips into same-width groups, and store them in individual bins marked with the appropriate strip width. Here are some of the advantages of storing scrap strips in your favorite widths.

Many quilt designs, such as the Nine-Patch, Four-Patch, Irish Chain, Log Cabin, Rail Fence, and others all start with rotary-cut strips. When you begin going through your collection of scraps, you may find that you have already gathered a sizeable number of cut strips that are ready to use in one of these kinds of quilts.

Strips are easy to store because they lie flat and do not get wrinkled or distorted easily when they are stacked. Wide strips can always be cut into narrower strips to suit the needs of the projects you want to make. You can cut strips into other shapes quickly and easily, including squares, 90-degree triangles, or equilateral triangles, whenever a project calls for them. You can keep adding strips to your scrap bins with each new project you make. For example, whenever I finish cutting strips from a certain fabric and have only a small piece of fabric left, I cut it into the widest strips possible, so that I have the option of cutting other shapes or strip widths from them in the future. This process does not add much time to any project, and it will help you build a large and versatile supply of ready-to-use strips for future quilts.

SQUARES

When you have a lot of oddly shaped pieces of leftover fabric, cut them into different sizes of squares, starting with the largest size square you can get from each scrap. You can always cut these larger squares into smaller squares (or triangles) in the future. To determine the sizes of squares you want to store on a regular basis, think about the sizes you most often use in your quilts. I like to keep bins of 2", 2½", 3", 3½" and 4" squares, because they fit easily into the quilt designs I like to make. If you have a strip in one of these widths, you can either cut it into squares immediately, or store it in your bins for future use.

In addition to cutting the largest size square possible from a scrap fabric, it is also very helpful to determine the smallest size square you like to work with in your quilts and make it a rule of thumb not to cut any squares smaller than that size. I do not cut squares any smaller than 2", because I can easily cut smaller squares from narrower strips, if I ever need them. This guideline isn't always easy to follow when faced with very small pieces of leftover fabric, but try not to let yourself be tempted to cut up every single bit of leftover fabric. If you have a quilting friend who loves making miniature quilts, consider donating these very small scraps to her. (Of course, if you *are* that person, then go for it – and keep even the tiniest scrap fabrics in a mini-bin!)

TRIANGLES

In addition to storing squares sorted by color in individual bins, you can also cut 90-degree triangles from oddly shaped fabrics that do not lend themselves easily to cutting squares. I like to cut 2⅞" and 3⅞" triangles, because these sizes are great for making 2" and 3" finished half-square triangle units.

Whatever shapes or strip widths you decide to cut, keep a set of acrylic rulers in various widths and shapes at your cutting table so that you have the one you need whenever you want it. See Resources on page 127 for my favorite brand. If you can't find a ruler in the exact size or shape you need, go to a glass and window store and have Plexiglas cut to your specifications.

FOLDED SCRAP FABRICS

Scraps that measure less than ¼ yard or strips that measure 3"- 6"-wide can be folded and stacked in drawers. Make sure there is a nice fold on one side of each large scrap, and stack pieces with the folds facing up, so each fabric is easily visible and easy to remove when you need it. This also helps to keep raw edges from fraying.

After washing and ironing any fabric, fold it from selvage to selvage. Then bring the fold to the selvage and fold the fabric accordion-style. Finally, fold the end of the fabric around the entire piece.

Store the folded fabrics on shelves, with the folds visible from the front, so that each fabric is easily recognizable. That way you can simply remove a fabric from the shelf, unfold it, and begin rotary cutting. If you have fabric left over, you can envelop it with the last fold again and put it back on the shelf.

If you have cupboards with doors that can be devoted to fabric storage, you can keep sun fading to a minimum. A closet in an extra bedroom also works well for keeping precious quilt fabrics out of direct sunlight.

OTHER CREATIVE STORAGE METHODS

Be creative in the way you choose to store your scrap fabrics. Explore some of the following ideas and decide which might work best for you.

• In office supply stores, you can find stackable bins that form towers of drawers. The drawers are usually removable, too, which makes them easy to place next to your sewing machine whenever you want a selection of scraps nearby.

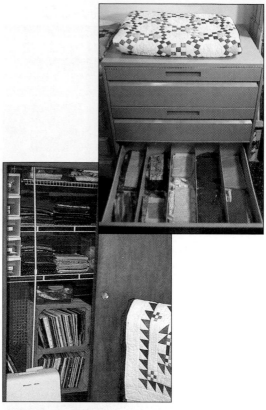

When you store fabrics in a closet, use a full-spectrum light bulb in the socket, or place a floor lamp nearby so you can easily see your fabrics.

• File cabinets come with dividers that can be adjusted for larger or smaller scraps.

• Bedroom closets can be turned into great fabric storage areas by installing commercial closet organizing systems.

SETTING UP A SEWING SPACE

Whether you have a large or a small sewing space, organize and equip it so that your sewing time is both productive and enjoyable. Consider the space you have available, your family's needs, and the amount of time and money you wish to spend setting up your work area. I work in a portion of my family room, because I always have little children with me during the day. They can play nearby whenever I am sewing, which works beautifully for me. As I was working on one of the quilts in this book, my four-year-old daughter liked to sit on my lap and pick out the strip or square that I should use next (which meant that I had no trouble making a scrap quilt that matched too much). One of the most precious memories of making that quilt will always be my daughter Kitty choosing the fabrics. Consider the following ideas, and see which ones best fit your quiltmaking needs.

• Look for a place where you can set up your sewing machine and leave it up at all times. If you have a whole room you can devote to quiltmaking, you can make that your personal domain of creativity. If not, be creative! Consider converting a bedroom closet to a sewing space. It is amazing how much you can accomplish in even short segments of time when you can sit down and start sewing immediately.

• If your sewing machine is heavy but must be put away between sewing sessions, keep it on a table that has wheels so you can roll it wherever you want to work. Your iron and ironing board are a vital part of your quiltmaking space, so find an ironing place easily accessible, near your sewing machine, and close to an outlet.

• Keep a flannel design wall in or near your workspace so that you can evaluate various aspects of making a quilt. You can tack flannel over a large piece of cardboard and fold it accordion-style for easy storage in a closet or underneath a bed.

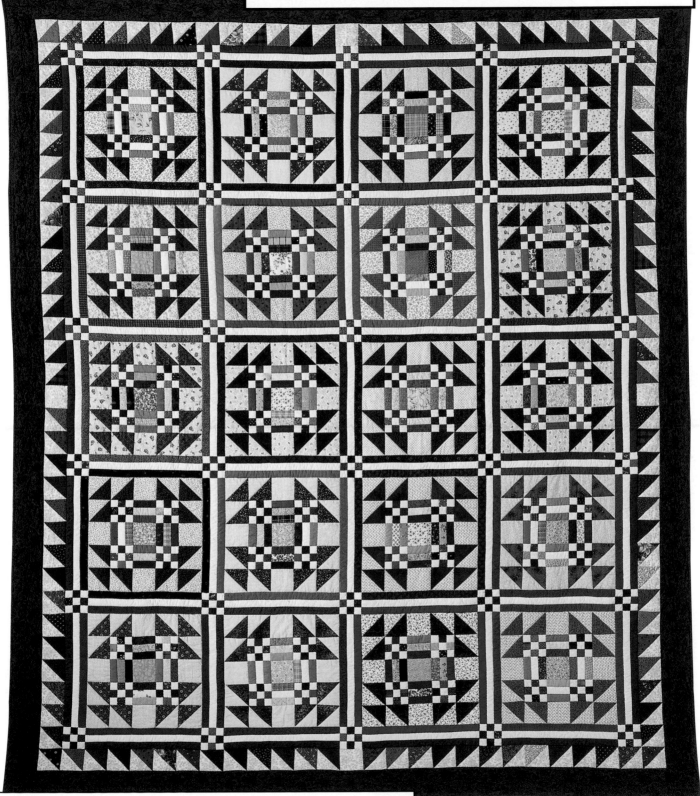

Geese of Many Colors 89" x 107"
Machine pieced and quilted by DeLoa Jones
Wanting to make a really scrappy version of this quilt, I used about anything that I had on hand. I kept the points the same colors and matched the rail fence sashing to the blocks they were next to in order to create a distinctive scrap color combination.

CREATING STRUCTURED LOOKS

My FRIENDS AMONG THE STARS quilt has a very scrappy look. The very light background fabric contrasts greatly with the scrap fabrics, giving it a structured look as well.

In my SCRAPPY STARS quilt, the values of the background fabric and the fabrics in the blocks are closer in value, producing a subtler scrap look.

FRIENDS AMONG THE STARS

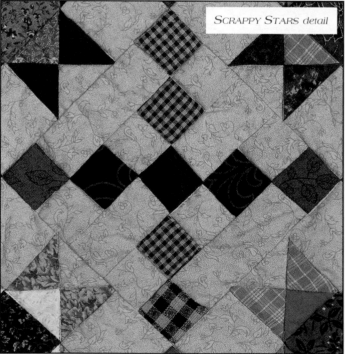

SCRAPPY STARS detail

FEATURING A DOMINANT COLOR

Some scrap quilts have a not-so-scrappy look because they contain one strong color that is dominant which pulls the whole design together. In my GOOSE IN THE POND AT DAWN quilt on page 13, the Nine-Patches within the blocks feature many different colors, but pink is the dominant color because of the placement of pinks in similar values in the surrounding triangles and in the triangles in the border.

USING DIFFERENT COLORS IN REPEAT BLOCKS

A scrap quilt that features the same blocks done in different colors also creates a scrappy look, without the randomness that comes from placing just any fabrics next to each other. This approach lets you control the colors you place together and feature a wide array of different fabrics within the same basic color scheme. My ALWAYS A FARMER'S DAUGHTER quilt on page 13 is a good example of this.

The same is true for my AUTUMN GLORY: STEPPING WITH THE STARS quilt on page 13, where the stars are made in many different color combinations. The design is pulled together by the bold, multicolored "stepping stones" in the alternate blocks.

WORKING WITH PARTICULAR PALETTES

When you work within specific color palettes, you can create different effects with your color choices, even in the same quilt design. The SUMMER BLOSSOMS quilt on page 13, made by Sandy Moon, has a light, summery feel because of its gentle flower colors and bright, leafy greens.

In my AUTUMN IN FULL BLOOM quilt on page 13, the filler blocks are all the same pieced pattern, yet they each feature slightly different color combinations and color values, while staying within a color palette that relates to the autumn season.

GOOSE IN THE POND AT DAWN

SUMMER BLOSSOMS *detail*

ALWAYS A FARMER'S DAUGHTER

AUTUMN IN FULL BLOOM *detail*

AUTUMN GLORY: STEPPING WITH THE STARS

WINTER detail

In WINTER, Corinne Wade chose to work with a cool palette of blues and whites, to express the feeling of a cold, clear winter sky.

For my CHRISTMAS IN FULL BLOOM quilt, a palette of bright reds and bold, dark greens were perfect for creating a festive, holiday scrap quilt.

When I chose the colors for my SPRING IN FULL BLOOM quilt, I wanted the palette to contain bright blues, purples, and pinks that would evoke the look of flowers blooming in the first rush of spring sunshine.

When you are searching for just the right fabric to fit a particular color scheme, remember to look through all of your scrap bins first. If you don't have enough of the right color in your collection of 2"-wide strips, simply go to your 2½"-wide strips – you can always cut them down to the size you need.

CHRISTMAS IN FULL BLOOM detail

COORDINATING WITH HOME DECOR

It is easy and enjoyable to make a scrap quilt that matches the colors in a room. Choose scrap fabrics that coordinate with the wallpaper, carpet, paint, and furniture in that room, and your finished wallhanging is bound to look great.

SPRING IN FULL BLOOM detail

VARYING COLORS AND VALUES

Value (the lightness or darkness of a color) is a very important element in selecting colors for a scrap quilt. Make it a habit to include a wide variety of light, medium, and dark fabrics in your color palette, so that the finished quilt will have greater visual interest. When I made the WHIRLWIND: CURVED LOG CABIN quilt at right, I wanted it to have a very scrappy, unplanned look, so I chose many different colors and values of each color. I placed blue-reds and orange-reds next to each other, included a bright yellow for pizazz, and mixed browns with blues for a truly scrappy look.

Make sure that there is enough contrast between the value of your background fabric(s) and the other scrap fabrics in your quilt to keep the pattern easily discernible. In the middle right photo, the samples blend together visually, because the values and color are too similar. This can create "holes" or interruptions in a quilt pattern.

In other parts of this quilt, a greater level of contrast in color and value make the pieces stand out against each other nicely, which will help keep a quilt pattern from being visually interrupted.

You can use color value intentionally to create secondary patterns within a quilt design. In LEAH'S GARDEN PATH quilt shown at right, a Pinwheels All Around pattern, the placement of the lights and darks creates an alternate, crisscross pattern. I have found that the way you place the values of your scrap fabrics has actually more visual impact than the colors themselves, so for each of the projects in this book, you will find suggestions for using color value creatively to enhance the patterns.

WHIRLWIND: CURVED LOG CABIN

LEAH'S GARDEN PATH

CHAPTER 3: SCRAP QUILT TECHNIQUES

The following techniques are used for making the projects in Chapter 4. In addition to being valuable timesavers, these helpful tips, tricks, and techniques will make your quiltmaking easier and more fun.

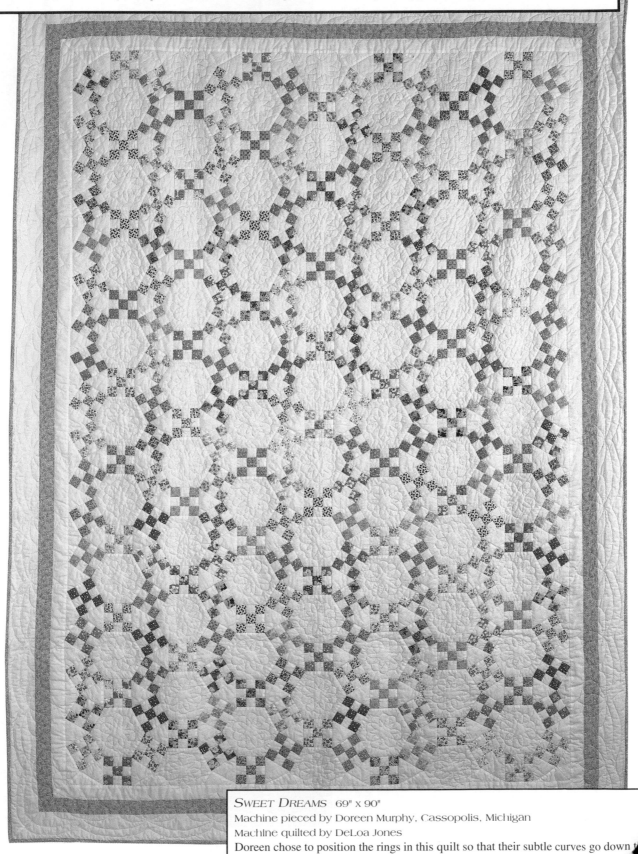

SWEET DREAMS 69" x 90"
Machine pieced by Doreen Murphy, Cassopolis, Michigan
Machine quilted by DeLoa Jones
Doreen chose to position the rings in this quilt so that their subtle curves go down the sides, rather than across the quilt and used a palette of '30s fabrics to create a real vintage look.

MACHINE PIECING

MATCHING AND PINNING TIPS

The following are some of my favorite tips for properly matching and pinning pieces, units, and blocks for making a patchwork quilt. Refer to this section often as you read through the various techniques explained on the following pages.

• For starters, consider investing in a package of silk pins that are approximately 1¼" long. They slide easily through fabric, without the thickness of regular pins, which makes all of your piecing more accurate.

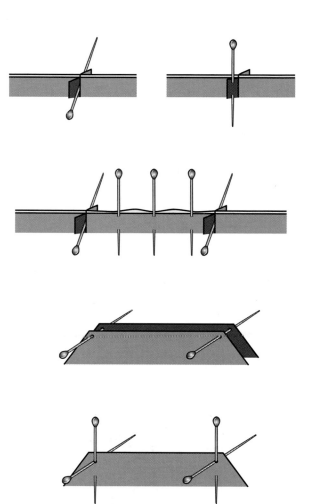

• To match an intersection where two units come together, insert a pin through both seam lines, exactly where they should match. Then insert another through the seam allowance on top to hold it in place, remove the first pin, and the seam will be ready to sew.

• For units that don't quite match up, let your sewing machine help ease in the excess fabric. First, match and pin at the intersections, and then place another pin in the middle of the unit to help distribute the excess evenly. Feel free to add more pins to reduce puckering, and sew this seam with the larger side next to the feed dogs on your sewing machine. The feed dogs will help to distribute the excess evenly, without puckers.

• For inset seams, insert a pin directly through the dots marked on the seam lines of the two pieces you want to sew together. (Make sure that your pins are straight, and not tilted in any way, which can make this process difficult.) Insert a second pin perpendicular to the seam line at each end of the seam, and then remove the two first pins. By doing this, you will make sure that your seams match precisely.

PRESSING GUIDELINES

Pressing is a very important part of making a quilt. The more accurate your pressing, the more accurate your finished quilt top will be. Try these tips for pressing success.

• Use a dry iron on a high heat setting to press pieces, units, or blocks.

• Press frequently as you piece, taking care not to distort the fabric.

• To press pieced strips without distorting them, first "set" the seams by laying the strip with the darker fabric on top, and pressing it.

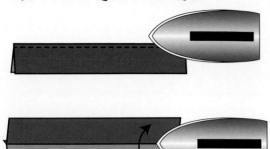

• After you "set" the seam on two sewn strips, open up the strips and gently press them again from the top. This will make the seam allowance fall naturally toward darker fabric. As you press, allow the heat of the iron to press the seam, rather than pushing on the seam with your iron.

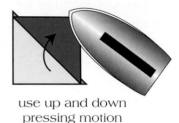

• For half-square triangle units, lay them so that the darker fabric is facing up on your ironing board, and "set" your seam by simply placing the iron on top of the unit. Then use your fingers to open up the fabrics, and gently finger-crease the seam. Press the seam gently with an iron, allowing the heat of the iron to press the seam.

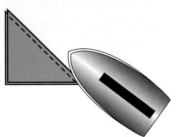

use up and down
pressing motion

• Overlap several of these units on your ironing board slightly, as you press. That way, when you press the top unit, the others underneath will get more heat. This makes it easier and faster to press the units one after the other.

• Some pieces, units, or blocks have bias edges that need to be pressed in a special manner. Finger-crease pieces with bias edges gently, after you sew each seam. This amount of pressing is sufficient for bias edges. If you feel that you really must use an iron, move it in a straight up-and-down motion as you press, rather than sliding it across the fabrics with bias edges. After you sew pieces or units with bias edges onto the next piece or unit, you can then press the unit as you would a half-square triangle unit.

• When your quilt top is assembled, press it with steam, taking care to avoid wrinkling or distortions.

• If you plan to machine quilt your project, you can press your completed quilt top with spray starch or spray sizing to give it added crispness.

• If you want to hand quilt, avoid using spray starch or sizing, which can make hand quilting more difficult.

QUICK CORNER TRIANGLES

The following piecing technique will enable you to add a triangle to the corner of a larger square, without the use of templates.

1. Draw a diagonal line from corner to corner on the smaller square that will become the corner triangle. Place it on the larger square, with right sides together, and sew on the diagonal line.

2. Trim the fabric at the corners, leaving a ¼" seam allowance from the sewing line, and press the corner triangle open.

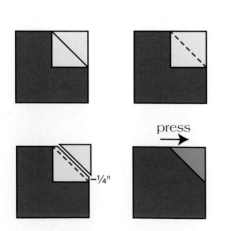

press

—¼"

HALF-SQUARE TRIANGLE UNITS

This technique is great for making scrap quilts because it makes it so easy to produce half-square triangle units that are the same size as other squares you are using.

1. Place two squares right sides together. Draw a diagonal line from corner to corner on the top square.

2. Sew exactly on the marked diagonal line.

3. Trim the fabric at the upper right corner, leaving a ¼" seam allowance from the sewn line. Press the seam allowance toward the darker fabric.

4. If you find that your half-square unit is smaller than your original squares, check your pressing to make sure you have not created any wrinkles or distortions in the fabric. If that doesn't solve the problem, you can take out the seam and sew it again, this time slightly to one side of the drawn line on the side where you will cut the seam allowance.

2-IN-1 HALF-SQUARE TRIANGLE UNITS

Here is an efficient way to sew two half-square triangle units quickly and easily, without cutting any triangles. Simply add ⅞" to the desired size of your finished square, and cut as many squares as you need in this size. (Remember that you will get two half-square triangle units from each pair of squares.)

1. Place two squares right sides together, and draw a diagonal line from corner to corner on the lighter fabric. Sew ¼" away from this line on both sides.

2. Rotary cut on the diagonal line between the two seams and press the seam allowances toward the darker fabric. Trim away the tiny triangles that peek out at the edges of each seam.

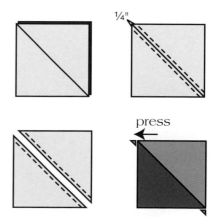

3. By chain-piecing these units, you can save even more time! Simply feed the pieces through your machine, sewing each seam on the left of the line, and then turn the whole chain around and sew the seams on the other side of the line.

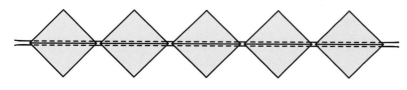

HOURGLASS UNITS

The following quick-piecing method helps to eliminate working with triangles and bias edges when making hourglass units. You will need to cut squares that are 1¼" larger than the size of your finished unit size. Each pair of squares that you sew together will yield two hourglass units.

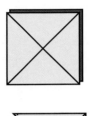

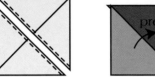

1. Place two squares right sides together. On the lighter square, draw diagonal lines from corner to corner in both directions.

2. Sew ¼" on each side of one of the marked diagonal lines.

3. Rotary cut directly on the drawn line between the seams, creating two half-square triangle units, and press the seam allowances toward the darker fabric.

4. Place the two half-square triangle units right sides together, with the colors in opposite positions and the seam allowances facing in opposite directions.

5. Extend the diagonal line marked on the lighter fabric across the dark triangle, and sew a seam ¼" on each side of this line. Rotary cut these units directly on the marked line, between the seams, and press these seam allowances open.

STRIP-PIECING

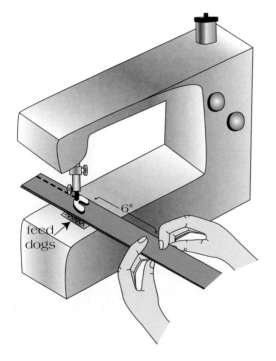

When you sew two strips together, the feed dogs of your sewing machine pull up on the bottom strip, while the presser foot pushes down on the top strip. This can create distortions in a finished seam. Try my finger-pinning for greater accuracy in strip-piecing. As you begin sewing two strips together, position the two strips together accurately and hold them with your fingers, approximately 6" in front of the needle. Sew until your fingers almost reach the presser foot, and stop. Pick up the strips again and align them for 6" more in front of the needle and sew that distance. Repeat this process until the entire strip is sewn. This allows you to be sure that you are feeding the two strips evenly through your sewing machine.

INSET SEAMS

When you need to set one piece into an angle between two other pieces, use the following technique.

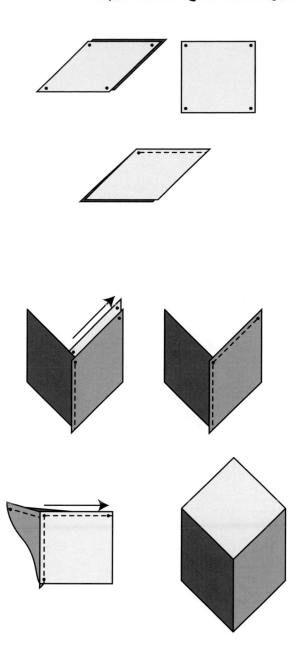

1. Start by marking a dot ¼" in from each corner of each piece.

2. Sew the two diamond shapes together, beginning at a ¼" dot, doing a few tiny backstitches to secure the seam, and sew to the other end of the fabric with a regular stitch length.

> To backstitch without adding a lot of bulk at the beginning of a seam, start a few stitches in front of the ¼" dot, backstitch to the dot, using a tiny stitch length. Then return to your regular stitch length and sew the rest of the seam.

3. To insert the square into the angle between the two joined diamond shapes, place the square underneath the joined diamonds with right sides together. Match the corner dot on the square to the point where the diamonds meet. Insert the needle exactly at that point, do a few short stitches or backstitch to secure the ends of the seam; then continue sewing to the end of the fabric.

4. Turn the pieces and sew the final seam, starting exactly at the point where the three pieces join, and continuing outward to the other edge of the square.

> When sewing inset seams, you will often be working with bias edges. By making it a practice to sew from the dot at the angle outward to the edges of the piece you are setting in, there is less chance of creating puckers at the angle where the seams meet. Also, if there are any bias edges on the bottom of the two fabrics you're sewing together, the motion of the feed dogs on your machine will help to eliminate any puckers at the angle.

CHAIN PIECING

Every quilter should add chain piecing to his or her repertoire of skills. It is a great way to sew pieces together quickly and allows you to conserve both time and thread. Normally, sewing two pieces together leaves a tail of thread approximately 6" long at both the beginning and the end of the seam, for a total of 12" wasted each time you sew two pieces together. The following technique will eliminate this waste and save you a lot of time as well.

Start by placing two pieces right sides together and feed them through your sewing machine. As you begin sewing, hold both threads taut, so that they do not get pulled into the throat plate. After you finish sewing the first two pieces together, take a couple more stitches beyond the edge of the fabric.

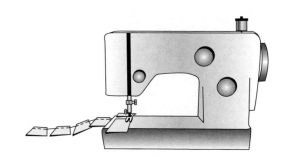

Then pick up two more pieces, place them right sides together, and feed them through the machine without lifting the presser foot. It is not necessary to backstitch at the end or beginning of each seam, because these seams will be secured later when you sew other pieces to them. Continue feeding pairs of pieces through your sewing machine in the same manner until you have sewn together the number of pairs you need. Then cut the pairs of pieces apart.

CHAIN-PIECING BLOCKS

This technique also offers the benefits of saving thread and time. In addition, piecing a block together chain-style means that you will only need to lay out the pieces and units for the block once. It also means that you won't position any of the pieces or units incorrectly as you sew or place a piece or unit in the wrong area of the block. Everything will automatically be "pinned together" as you sew.

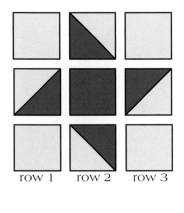

1. Start by laying out all of the pieces and units for a block on a flat surface. Designate a number for each of the rows in your block, starting on the left side, as shown.

2. Lay the pieces/units of row 2 on top of the pieces/units in row 1, with the right sides together.

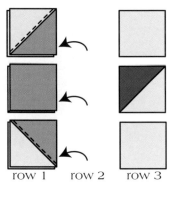

3. Starting with the top two pieces/units, sew each pair of pieces/units together. Continue sewing the row 1 and 2 pieces/units together in a chain. When you finish, open up the sewn pieces, but do not cut the threads between them yet.

4. Starting at the top again, lay the row 3 pieces/units on top of the row 2 pieces/units, and sew them together chain-style, as before.

5. You have now sewn all of the vertical seams in the three rows, creating three horizontal rows that are "pinned together" by the threads between them.

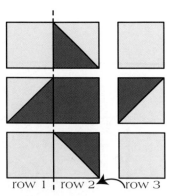

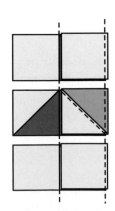

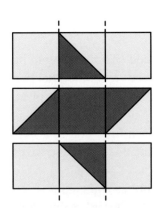

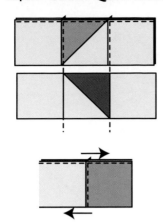

6. At this point, check your block again and make sure that everything is in the correct position for the pattern. Sew the first two horizontal rows together by placing the top row onto the middle row.

7. As you sew the rows of your block together, try to make sure that the direction of the seam allowances between pieces or units alternate so that you can get a tight intersection where they meet. I also suggest pressing the seam allowances between rows in opposite directions, unless a particular light or dark fabric needs to be pressed differently.

Chain-piecing a block together is easy, if you follow a couple of simple rules. First, make it a habit to flip the pieces or units in one row onto the ones in the previous row, as if you were turning a page in a book (in other words, flip the pieces or units from right to left). Second, whenever you pick up two pieces or units you want to sew together, hold the edge that you want to sew between your thumbs and forefingers; otherwise, it can be very easy to end up sewing the wrong edges together. By handling pieces or units in this way, you will always be assured that you are sewing the correct edges together.

NEEDLE-TURN APPLIQUÉ

Use the following needle-turn appliqué technique for stitching the appliqué shapes in the projects in this book.

MAKING TEMPLATES

Trace the templates for the appliqué shapes in your project onto template plastic and cut them out. Mark around each template on the right side of the appropriate fabric. As you cut out each shape, add a ¼" seam allowance by eye.

THE APPLIQUÉ STITCH

1. Use a straight pin to pin each appliqué shape in the appropriate place on the quilt top.

2. Thread a size #11 sharp needle with thread that matches the fabric in your appliqué and bring it up just inside the marked turning line of the appliqué shape. Use the tip and the shank of the needle to turn the seam allowance under gently, so that the marked turning line is just out of sight for approximately ½" to 1".

3. To begin stitching, insert the needle into the background fabric, right next to the spot where the thread comes out of the appliqué shape. Bring the needle back up through the background fabric, and catch the very tip of the fold on the appliqué shape.

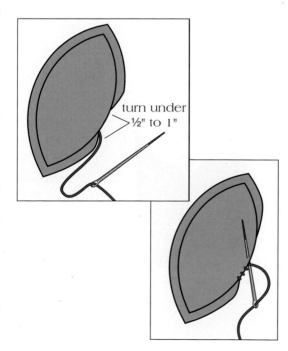

turn under ½" to 1"

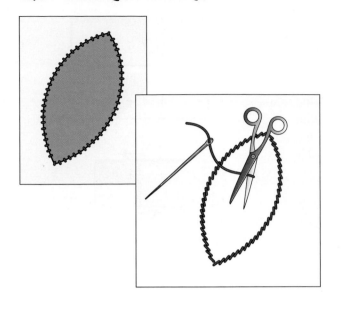

4. Pull the thread all the way through, and repeat this process until you have stitched the entire appliqué shape onto the background fabric of your quilt top.

5. To end a thread, insert the needle through the background fabric and pull it all the way through. Wind the thread around the needle two or three times, and insert it through the background fabric only; bring it out again approximately ¼" to ½" away, taking care to stay inside your stitched lines. Pull the thread through, creating a small knot on the surface of the background fabric. Tug on the thread until this knot pops through the fabric and lodges between your stitched appliqué shape and the background fabric. Clip thread close to the background fabric.

> For appliquéing steep outer curves, turn under only about ¼" of the seam allowance at a time. For deep inner curves, make clips into the seam allowance before you stitch, spacing the clips approximately ⅛" to ¼" apart.

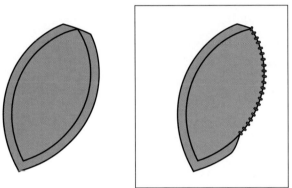

OUTER POINTS

1. For outer points, like those on a leaf, start by turning under the seam allowance at the very tip of the point.

2. Turn under the seam allowance on the right side of the leaf and stitch up to the point. Take an extra stitch at the very point to enhance its sharpness, before continuing to stitch the other side of the leaf.

> For a great way to avoid getting your thread tangled around straight pins while you appliqué, try glue-basting your appliqués in place, using the kind of glue that comes in a small bottle with a very fine needle tip (see Resources, page 127). Place small dots of glue on the back sides of your appliqué pieces and position them wherever you want on your background fabric. The glue is water-based and will wash out after you finish stitching.

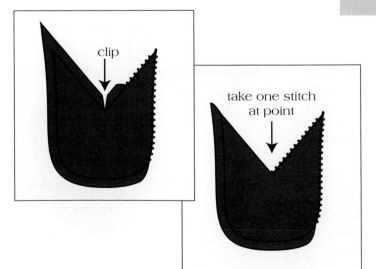

INNER POINTS

1. Stitch to approximately ¼" from an inner point. Make a clip to the inner point, and stitch the remaining distance to the point.

2. Take one extra stitch to reinforce the inner point and then turn under the seam allowance on the next side of the inner point. Continue stitching the remainder of the shape to the background fabric.

PERFECT CIRCLES

1. Perfect circles are easy to appliqué if you start by doing a row of gathering stitches about ⅛" in from the edge of the fabric.

2. Place a cardboard or heat-resistant templar template in the middle of the circle and pull the thread to draw the fabric around the template.

3. Press the circle appliqué with the templar circle or cardboard template still inside it; then remove the template and press it again. The circle is now ready to stitch on your background fabric.

Use a little spray starch to hold the fabric in place while pressing circle appliqués.

insert a template before gathering

PREPARING STEMS AND VINES

1. Cut stems or vines for the projects in this book on the bias to make it easy to stitch their curves. Each bias strip should be twice the desired width of your finished stem or vine plus ½" for seam allowances.

2. Fold the bias strip in half lengthwise, with the wrong sides together, and stitch a seam ¼" in from the raw edges.

3. Trim the seam allowance to ⅛" and press the bias strip so that the seam allowance is centered on one side. The bias strip is now ready to stitch in place as a stem or vine.

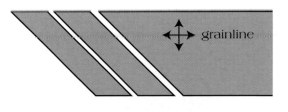

grainline

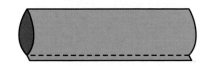

Bias pressing bars make the process of pressing stems or vines much simpler. Just slide a bias pressing bar in the appropriate size into your sewn stem or vine, making sure that the seam allowance is centered on the wrong side, and press. The bias stem or vine is now ready to stitch on your background fabric.

FINISHING TOUCHES

The way you treat the wrong side of your finished appliqué will affect the way the front side looks. If you want your finished work to lie as flat and smooth as patchwork, trim away the background fabric underneath the appliqué shapes, taking care to cut ¼" inside your stitching lines. Simply cut a small slit in the background fabric only, and carefully trim away the background fabric ¼" inside your stitched lines. If you want your finished appliqué to have a bit more visual dimension, leave the background fabric intact.

ASSEMBLING A QUILT TOP

The following techniques will enable you to assemble a quilt top so that it lies flat, with corners that are straight and true.

JOINING QUILT CENTER

Refer to the project instructions for joining the blocks, sashing strips, or other units of your project together to create the quilt center for your quilt.

ADDING THE BORDERS

Whether you decide to add pieced borders to your quilt or use straight strips of fabric, take extra care when you attach them to the quilt center so that your finished quilt top will lie straight and true, with no rippled or wavy edges.

STRAIGHT BORDERS

If your border strips are slightly larger than the quilt center, the result will be a quilt top that has wavy edges. If your border strips are slightly smaller than the quilt center, the quilt center will become distorted. Careful measuring can eliminate both problems.

1. Start by measuring your quilt top vertically through the middle, parallel to the sides. This will tell you the correct length to cut your side border strips.

2. Pin the side border strips to the center of your quilt, starting at the middle and matching the quarter points, to distribute the border fabric evenly along the sides of the quilt center. Add as many pins as you wish, and gently ease in any excess fabric in certain areas, if necessary.

To make it simple to ease in any extra fabric when you attach a border to your quilt center, sew this area with the looser side placed next to your feed dogs. This will help to distribute the excess evenly.

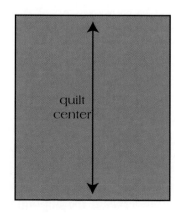

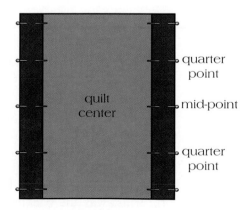

quarter point

mid-point

quarter point

3. Measure your quilt top through the middle, from side to side including the side borders you just attached. Cut the top and bottom border strips this length.

4. Pin the top and bottom border strips to the top and bottom edges of the quilt center, matching the center and quarter points, in the same manner as for the side border strips.

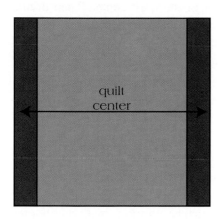

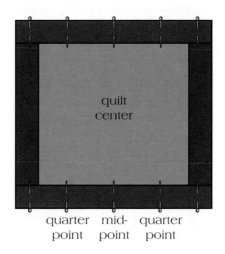

quarter   mid-   quarter
point   point   point

PIECED BORDERS

You will also need to measure your quilt center to ensure a good fit for pieced borders.

1. If your pieced borders are slightly longer than the measurements you take through your quilt center, you will need to adjust them to fit. It is easy to restitch a few seams, making them a little wider, as needed. The trick is to make sure that you widen a number of different seams slightly and spread them out evenly along the border seams, rather than making one seam quite a bit narrower, which would be noticeable.

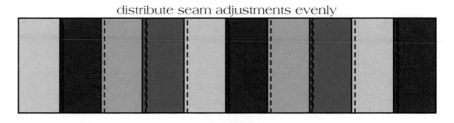

distribute seam adjustments evenly

2. If your pieced border is a bit smaller than the measurements you take through your quilt center, simply take some seams out and restitch them with a narrower seam allowance, taking care to distribute these evenly along the pieced border as before. If you adjust 16 seams by ¹⁄₁₆" each, (or about one thread width), you can reduce the length of your pieced border by a whole inch, almost invisibly.

MITERED CORNERS

If you want your borders to have mitered corners, you will also need to take a few measurements first, but in a different way than for straight or pieced borders.

1. Rather than measuring the quilt center from edge to edge, you will need to measure it from seam allowance to seam allowance in both directions. To do this, start by marking a dot ¼" in from the edge of the fabric at the corners and at the mid-point on each side of your quilt center and measure from center dot to center dot in both directions.

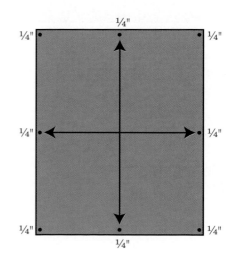

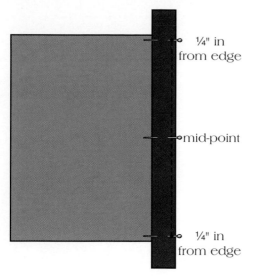

¼" in from edge

mid-point

¼" in from edge

2. You will need to add the length for the miter to this measurement in order to determine how long to cut your border strips. To calculate the length of the miter, multiply your border strip width times 2 and add 2" as a safety margin. Add this number to the measurement you took through the middle of your quilt center in both directions and cut your border strips to these lengths.

3. Pin a side border strip to the midpoint of the quilt center. Then divide the vertical measurement of your quilt top (from seam allowance to seam allowance) in half and place a pin on the border strip that distance from the center pin, on both sides. Match these pins to the quilt center, ¼" in from the edge. Add more pins along the rest of the border, easing in any excess fabric, if necessary. Sew this side border strip to the quilt center starting and stopping at the ¼" marks.

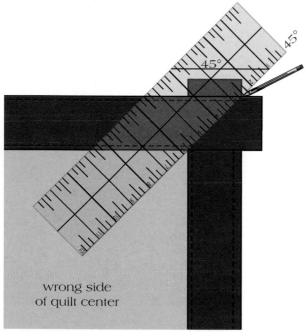

45°

45°

wrong side of quilt center

4. Pin and sew an adjacent border strip to the quilt center in the same manner as for the side border strip, starting and stopping exactly ¼" in from the corners so that the adjacent seams meet. Lay your quilt top face down on a flat surface. Working with one border strip at a time, mark a line at a 45-degree angle, extending from the ¼" corner point outward to the edge of the border strip. This line must be accurate, so check your ruler in several places before drawing these lines for the mitered corner seams. Mark both border strips at each corner of your quilt.

5. Fold your quilt top so the right sides of two adjacent borders are facing each other. Pin the borders together, matching the marked mitering lines. Mitering a corner border seam is just like sewing any other inset seam. Starting at the ¼" corner dot of the border, sew outward to the outer corner of the border, backstitching at both ends of this seam.

6. Open up the border and lay the quilt on a floor to check that the mitered seam lies flat. If you check a mitered corner seam with the quilt placed on a table, the weight of the quilt can pull it over the edge of the table, and the mitered seam may not be easy to check. When you are happy with the mitered corner seam, fold the quilt again so that the borders face each other and rotary cut the excess fabric from the seam. Press the mitered corner seam open.

wrong side of quilt center

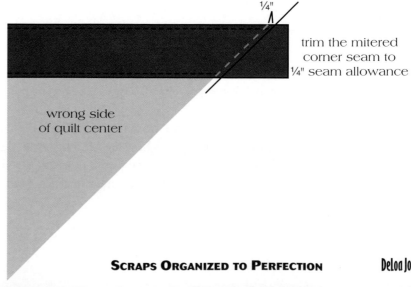

¼"

trim the mitered corner seam to ¼" seam allowance

wrong side of quilt center

7. Repeat Steps 3 through 6 for the remaining three border corners of your quilt top.

8. If your border features two or more strips of fabric sewn together lengthwise, you can sew all of the strips for each border together before you add them to the quilt top. If you take this approach, remember that each individual border must extend over the previous one by at least the same amount as its width, in order to allow enough fabric for mitering the corner seams. To be safe, add an extra 1" to each of these measurements so you don't end up short of fabric when you mark the mitering lines at each corner of your quilt top. You can always trim any excess away.

offset border strips to allow for mitered corner seams

9. For a border like this, mark the mitering lines just as you would mark them for single border strips. When you match the adjacent corner seam lines, remember that you will also need to make sure the seams of the different border strips meet each other. Then, simply sew the mitered corner seams and trim them as before.

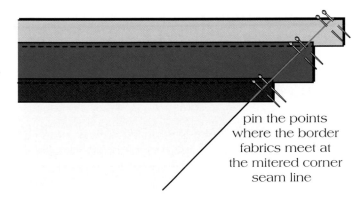

pin the points where the border fabrics meet at the mitered corner seam line

QUILTING

Follow these steps to prepare a quilt sandwich for quilting by hand or machine.

PREPARING THE BACKING

The backing for a quilt should be 2" to 4" larger on each side than the quilt top itself. There are a couple of reasons for adding this extra width. First, quilting draws the three layers of a quilt together along your stitching lines, creating shrinkage. As a rule of thumb, the thicker your batting, the more

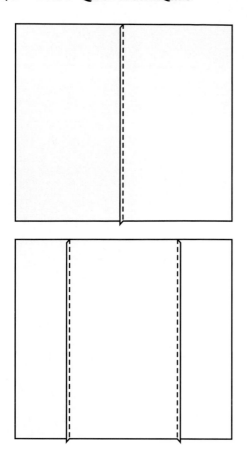

shrinkage there will be in your finished quilt. If the backing, batting, and quilt top start out the same size, the edges may not be even when you finish quilting. Also, the extra fabric and batting around the sides of a quilt sandwich enable you to place borders in a hoop or insert the quilt into the frame easily for hand quilting.

You can sew a backing that features a single seam down the middle, or two seams that are offset. Just make sure to trim away the selvages before you sew the pieces together, so their tight edges will not pucker the seams in your backing or make hand quilting difficult.

> Piecing a backing can also be a very interesting way to finish a quilt. Try sewing odd pieces together from your stash for a scrappy backing.

MARKING METHODS

Preparing a completed quilt top for hand or machine quilting deserves as much care and attention as every other step in the quiltmaking process. You can mark quilting designs directly onto light fabrics, or if your quilt contains mostly dark fabrics, you can trace quilting designs onto paper, enhance the lines by going over them with a black permanent marker, tape the paper on top of a light box, and lay your finished quilt top over the paper to mark the designs. Here are two of my favorite tools for marking quilting designs for hand or machine quilting.

Chalk pencils show up nicely on both light and dark fabrics, and the marks are easy to remove after you finish quilting. These types of pencils should be stored lying flat, so that the chalk inside will remain in one piece. When you mark quilting designs with a chalk pencil, use a soft touch to avoid breaking the tip of the chalk, and sharpen these pencils often as you mark.

> Whenever you are considering purchasing a new marking tool, be sure to read the manufacturer's instructions on the packaging so that you are aware of any special properties of the marking substance or directions for using the tool properly.

Water-soluble blue marking pens leave sharp lines that are easy to see. However, the markings cannot be subjected to heat, which will often set the marks permanently. The heat of an iron or even the heat inside a car on a hot day can damage a quilt top marked with water-soluble pens. If you choose to use them, it is usually best to mark each design right before you quilt it, and remove the markings immediately with water, if possible.

> Whatever type of marking tool you use, it is a good idea to test it on scraps of fabric from your actual quilt top. That way you can determine how easy it is to remove the marks with water or a soft, clean cloth, before you mark your entire quilt top.

LAYERING AND BASTING

Layering the backing, batting and quilt top into a quilt "sandwich" will make it easy to quilt the quilt evenly, without puckering.

1. Tape the backing fabric right side down on a large, flat surface, such as two tables pushed together, or a clean floor. Taping the backing down secures it in place, so that it will not move when you adjust the positions of the batting and the quilt top.

2. Lay the batting on top of the taped backing fabric. Most packaged battings have folds that make it easy to unfold and position the batting evenly on top of the backing fabric.

3. Finally, position the quilt top over the batting with the right side facing up. Using a long needle, baste the backing, batting, and quilt top together in a grid-like fashion, spacing the grid lines approximately 6" – 8" apart. Begin at the middle of the quilt and work outward to each side and then toward the corners. Baste around the outside edges of the quilt sandwich, and it will be ready for hand quilting.

4. If you wish to machine quilt, you can pin-baste the layers of a quilt sandwich together. Simply layer the quilt as before, but use 1" safety pins to secure the layers together in a grid. There is some movement of a quilt when you close safety pins individually; to avoid this, insert all of the pins first and then go back and close them all at the same time, using a grapefruit spoon.

backing   batting   quilt top

6"–8" intervals

There are many different types and brands of hand quilting frames on the market now, which do not require basting. These feature three- or four-rail systems that allow the quilt backing, batting, and quilt top to roll independently onto a single rail during the quilting process. These types of floor frames can save you many hours of basting the layers of a quilt sandwich together.

HAND QUILTING

Follow these tips and the following steps for doing hand quilting stitches that will give your quilts beautiful visual texture.

Use size #8, #9, #10, or #12 "betweens" for hand quilting. These short needles will enable you to get small, even quilting stitches. You will need a metal thimble that has good indentations and a rim around the top, for controlling your needle as you quilt. You may wish to wrap the forefinger of the hand that holds the needle with self-adhesive finger wrap so you can pull the needle in and out of the quilt sandwich more easily. This tape is not bulky, and the stickiness of it helps to grab the needle. If finger wraps seem too bulky, you can also use finger cots which are both lightweight and sturdy, for

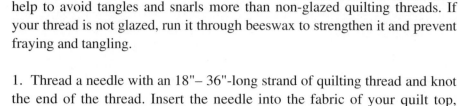

better needle traction. Use a quilting thread that has a glaze on it, which will help to avoid tangles and snarls more than non-glazed quilting threads. If your thread is not glazed, run it through beeswax to strengthen it and prevent fraying and tangling.

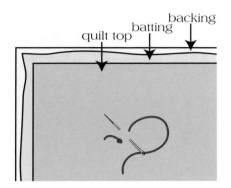

1. Thread a needle with an 18"– 36"-long strand of quilting thread and knot the end of the thread. Insert the needle into the fabric of your quilt top, allowing the knot to lodge inside the layer of batting. This is done by making a stitch only through the top layer of your quilt and pulling the knot through. If a knot is hard to pull through, insert the needle perpendicular to the knot, a little in front of it, as shown, and gently lift the quilt top as you pull on the thread. This will pop the knot through easily.

2. Insert the needle through the layers of the quilt sandwich, keeping it as close to vertical as possible, and feel the point of the needle with the index finger of your hand underneath the quilt sandwich.

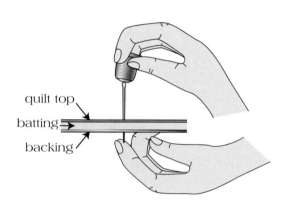

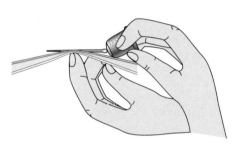

3. As soon as you feel the needle, rock it back up and bring it up through the three layers of the quilt sandwich again, completing the first stitch.

4. Rock the needle so that it is perpendicular to the quilt sandwich again, and insert it back down through the three layers to start the next stitch. Bring the needle back up through the three layers again to form a second stitch just like the first one. Continue rocking the needle and taking stitches until you have 4 or 5 stitches on the needle; then pull the thread all the way through the quilt sandwich. By putting several stitches on the needle at one time, the stitching lines on both the front and the back sides of your quilt will have a smoother, more even appearance.

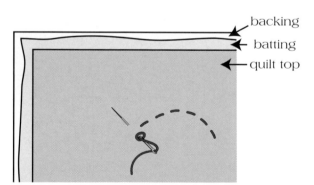

tug on thread to tighten it around needle
at the surface of the quilt top

5. To end a line of hand quilting stitches, knot the thread by winding it around the needle twice and insert the needle through the top fabric; bring the needle up again through the top fabric approximately ½" away and tighten the thread around needle at the surface of the fabric. Then you can simply pull the thread gently to pop the knot into the batting layer and clip the thread close to the surface of the fabric.

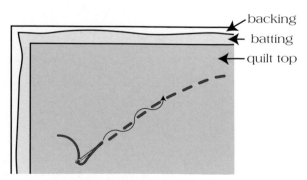

wind thread through batting
layer for 3–4 stitches

6. You can also end a line of quilting stitches by taking a backstitch on top of your final stitch, or by weaving the needle backward inside the batting layer, from side to side through three or four stitches. Bring the needle up again through the top fabric, draw the thread completely through, and clip it just above the surface of the fabric.

MACHINE QUILTING

Any of the projects in this book can be quilted by machine. If you are an experienced machine quilter, mark the designs you desire on your quilt top and machine stitch them, either by free-motion or machine-guided techniques. If you are new to machine quilting, check your local quilt shop for books on how to machine quilt or see the Bibliography on page 127.

FINISHING TECHNIQUES

Use the following methods to give your quilts final flourishing touches of perfection.

BINDING

A single-fold binding consists of one layer of fabric that goes around the edges of a quilt. It works very well for wallhangings that do not get much wear. The following instructions are for binding a quilt with a double-fold binding which is more durable and great for bed quilts or any type of quilt that will get a lot of wear. Each project in Chapter 4 lists the yardage needed for cutting 2⅝"-wide binding strips on the crosswise grain. When you cut the binding strips for your project, cut enough 2⅝" x 42" binding strips to go around the edges of your quilt, adding 10" extra to allow for mitering the corners and finishing the ends of the binding. Follow these steps to attach the binding to the edges of your quilt.

1. Place the short ends of the binding strips right sides together and sew them with a diagonal seam. Trim these seam allowances to ¼" and press them open so the binding lies flat. Then fold the entire binding in half lengthwise, with wrong sides together, and press.

Cut bias binding strips from an interesting plaid fabric to create an attractive edge finish for a quilt that features the same fabric in the patchwork or appliqué.

2. Open up the beginning of the binding and cut it to a 45-degree angle. Turn under and finger-press a ¼" seam allowance along the diagonal edge. Fold the binding in half again and position it along the edge of the quilt, starting away from a corner. Sew the outermost tip of the turned-under ¼" fold to the quilt. Then start sewing the binding to the quilt, beginning ½" from the other turned-under fold.

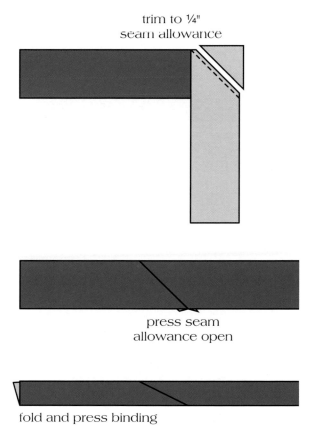

trim to ¼"
seam allowance

press seam
allowance open

fold and press binding

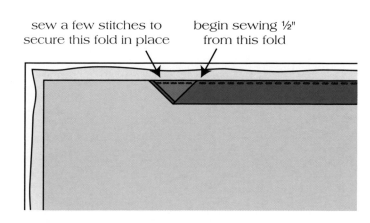

sew a few stitches to
secure this fold in place

begin sewing ½"
from this fold

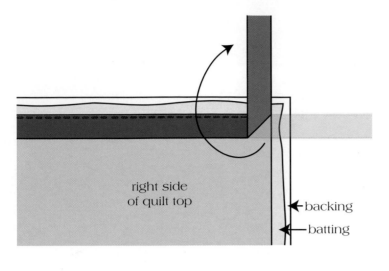

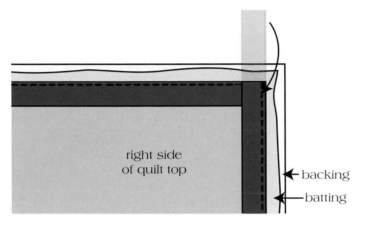

right side
of quilt top

◄backing

◄batting

right side
of quilt top

◄backing

◄batting

wrong side
of quilt

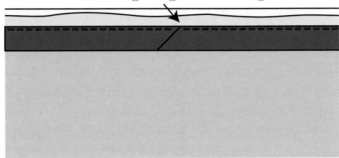

insert the end of the binding into the opening
at the beginning of the binding

3. Stitch up to ¼" from the first corner of your quilt and backstitch to secure the seam. Remove the quilt from your sewing machine and fold the binding up so that it is perpendicular to the quilt.

4. Fold the binding back down on top of itself so that the top fold is even with the raw edge of the previously stitched binding and begin stitching this side of the binding to the quilt top, starting at the fold. This will create a nice mitered corner in your finished binding.

5. Sew the binding to the remaining edges of the quilt in the same manner, stopping approximately 10" from the point where you started.

6. Insert the end of the binding into the opening at the beginning of the binding and sew the remainder of the binding seam through all layers.

7. Trim the excess batting and backing fabric even with the edges of the quilt top. If you wish to add a hanging sleeve to display your quilt on a wall, skip to "Attaching a Hanging Sleeve" on page 35 and add one at this point. Referring to "The Appliqué Stitch" on page 23, fold the binding to the back side of the quilt and stitch it in place, covering the machine stitching. At each corner, miter the binding by folding first one side then the other at a 45-degree angle. Hand-stitch the mitered corner folds in place.

If you have a walking- or even-feed foot for your sewing machine, use it to sew the binding to your quilt top, so that your binding seams will be smooth and free of puckers. You can also purchase a generic one that will fit your machine. Check your owner's manual to find out whether your machine has a high shank or a low shank, to make sure you get the right type of walking foot for your machine.

ATTACHING A HANGING SLEEVE

Follow these steps to make a sleeve for displaying a wall quilt.

1. Measure across the top of the quilt and subtract ½" from this measurement. Cut a strip of fabric 6" wide by that length. Turn under ¼" twice at each of the short ends of the strip and sew them in place by machine.

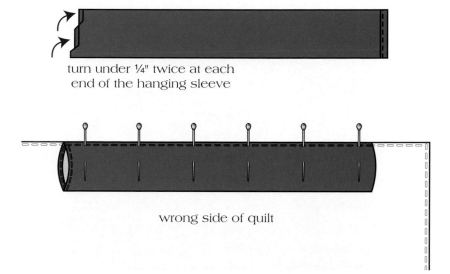

turn under ¼" twice at each
end of the hanging sleeve

2. After you have sewn the binding to your quilt by machine and trimmed the excess batting and backing even with the edges of the quilt top, fold the wrong sides of the hanging sleeve together and pin the raw edges in place along the top edge on the back side of your quilt. Sew the hanging sleeve to the quilt by machine, taking care to stay inside the binding seam.

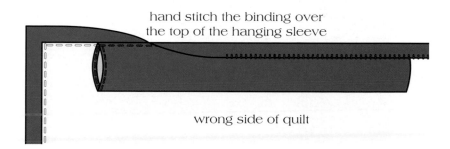

wrong side of quilt

3. Fold the binding to the back side of your quilt and hand stitch it in place over the top edge of the hanging sleeve, referring to "The Appliqué Stitch" on page 23.

hand stitch the binding over
the top of the hanging sleeve

wrong side of quilt

4. Fold the hanging sleeve up so that it reaches halfway across the width of the top binding. Smooth down a fold at the other long edge of the hanging sleeve and pin it in position on the back side of your quilt. Hand stitch the lower folded edge of the hanging sleeve to the backing fabric. This will allow enough ease so that your quilt will hang straight and flat against a wall.

You can also use a walking- or even-feed foot to attach a hanging sleeve to keep this seam pucker-free.

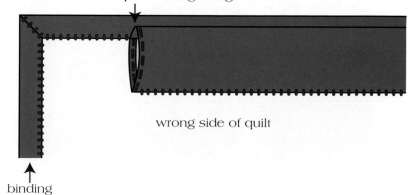

fold hanging sleeve up to create ease that
will allow the quilt to hang straight and flat

wrong side of quilt

binding

CHAPTER 4: PROJECTS

The quilts that follow are great designs for using up the many scrap strips, squares, triangles, and other shapes that seem to add up so quickly in your fabric stash. Or you can purchase fabric by the yard and create more structured color schemes; either way, the results will be spectacular-looking quilts!

PEACEFUL STARS 29" x 36"
Machine pieced and quilted by DeLoa Jones
I made this version of the Scrappy Stars pattern in some of my favorite colors, which creates a very matched look.

SCRAPPY STARS

The Ohio Star blocks in this wallhanging are great places to try out a variety of color combinations. Adding in some alternate Chain blocks with a scrappy look ties the whole design together. Don't let the small pieces intimidate you – the strip-piecing and hourglass techniques in Chapter 3 make this little quilt both quick and easy to piece.

FABRICS AND SUPPLIES

Note: If you are using pre-cut pieces from your scrap bins, refer to the Cutting List for the number and type of pieces to cut for this project.

¾ yard	background fabric for Ohio Star and Chain blocks
¼ yard	assorted dark fabrics for Ohio Star points
¼ yard	assorted contrast fabrics for Ohio Star centers
¼ yard	assorted light, medium, and dark fabrics for triangles around center squares
½ yard	assorted medium-to-dark fabrics for alternate Chain blocks
¼ yard	medium gold fabric for inner border
¾ yards	dark blue fabric for outer border and binding
1¼ yards	of fabric for backing
33" x 40"	piece of batting

FINISHED QUILT	29" x 36"
FINISHED BLOCK SIZE	approximately 5" square

CUTTING LIST

OHIO STAR BLOCKS

FROM THE BACKGROUND FABRIC:

Cut 12 squares	each 2⅞" x 2⅞" (1 per block)
Cut 48 squares	each 2⅛" x 2⅛" (4 per block)

FROM THE ASSORTED DARK FABRICS:

Cut 24 squares	each 2⅞" x 2⅞" (2 per block)

FROM THE ASSORTED LIGHT/MED/DARK FABRICS:

Cut 12 squares	each 2⅞" x 2⅞" (1 per block)

FROM THE ASSORTED CONTRAST FABRICS:

Cut 12 squares	each 2⅛" x 2⅛" (1 per block)

CHAIN BLOCKS

FROM THE BACKGROUND FABRIC:

Cut a 3½" x 42" strip.	
Cut 3 strips	each 1½" x 42".
Cut a 2½" x 42" strip.	

FROM THE MEDIUM-TO-DARK FABRICS:

Cut 6 strips	each 1½" x 42".

BORDERS AND BINDING

FROM THE MEDIUM GOLD FABRIC:

Cut 4 strips	each 1½" x 42".

FROM THE DARK BLUE FABRIC:

Cut 4 strips	each 3" x 42".
Cut 4 binding strips	each 2⅝" x 42".

PIECING THE OHIO STAR BLOCKS

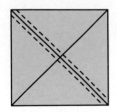

Note: The same background fabric is featured in all of the Ohio Star blocks. Choose a different dark fabric for the star points in each block. Choose a different light, medium, or dark fabric for the triangles around the center square. Choose a different contrast fabric for the center square in each block.

1. Mark a diagonal line from corner to corner in both directions on each of the twelve 2⅞" background squares. Also mark a diagonal line from corner to corner in both directions on the twelve 2⅞" light squares.

2. Place the twelve 2⅞" x 2⅞" background squares right sides together with twelve of the dark 2⅞" x 2⅞" squares. Also place twelve of the 2⅞" x 2⅞" light squares and twelve of the dark 2⅞" x 2⅞" squares right sides together.

3. On each pair of squares, sew a ¼" seam on both sides of one of the marked diagonal lines.

4. Rotary cut directly on the marked diagonal line between your stitching lines, separating each pair of squares, for a total of 24 background/dark half-square triangle units and 24 dark/light half-square triangle units. Trim the excess fabric at the corners of each unit and press the seam allowances toward the dark fabric.

5. Place a light/dark half-square triangle unit right sides together with a background/dark half-square triangle unit, with the seam allowances facing in opposite directions and the dark fabrics on opposite sides. Using a fabric-marking pen or pencil, extend the diagonal line from the light fabric to the dark half of the square. Repeat for all of the remaining pairs of half-square triangle units.

6. Sew a ¼" seam on both sides of the extended diagonal lines.

7. Rotary cut exactly on the marked diagonal line between your stitching lines, creating a total of 48 hourglass units for the star points. Trim the excess fabric at the corners of these units, and press the seam allowances toward the dark fabric.

8. For each Ohio Star block, lay out four hourglass units, four 2⅛" background squares and a 2⅛" contrast center star square. Referring to Chain-Piecing Blocks on page 21, sew the units for each Ohio Star block together into three vertical rows; then sew the vertical rows together to complete each block.

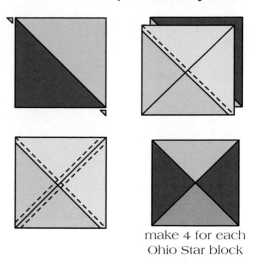

make 4 for each
Ohio Star block

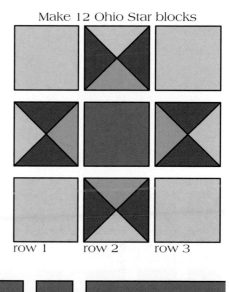

Make 12 Ohio Star blocks

row 1   row 2   row 3

STRIP-PIECING THE ALTERNATE CHAIN BLOCKS

Note: The same background fabric is featured in all of the alternate Chain blocks. Choose different medium-to-dark strips for making the strip sets.

1. Sew together two 1½" x 42" medium-to-dark strips with a 3½" x 42" background strip between them.

2. Press the seam allowances toward the medium fabrics and cut the strip sets into 1½" segments. You will need to cut a total of 26 of these segments: 12 for the alternate Chain blocks, 10 for the setting-triangle blocks, and 4 for the corner triangle blocks.

3. For the next step, you will need only to work with half strip lengths, so cut 1 medium 1½" x 42" strip in half and cut two 1½" x 42" light strips in half. Sew a strip set consisting of two 1½" x 22" medium strips and three 1½" light background strips.

4. Press the seam allowances toward the medium fabrics. Cut the strip set into twelve 1½"-wide segments.

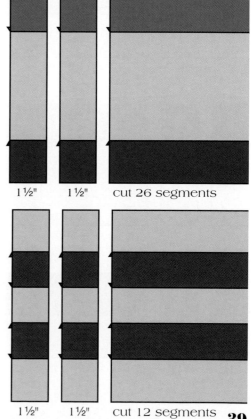

1½"   1½"   cut 26 segments

1½"   1½"   cut 12 segments

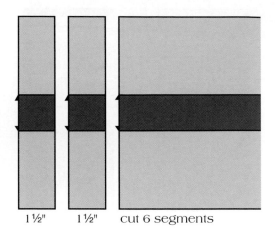

1½"   1½"   cut 6 segments

5. Cut a 2½" x 42" background strip into two 10" lengths and cut one 1½" x 22" medium strip into a 10" length. Sew the two 2½" x 10" background strips and the 1½" x 10" medium strip into a strip set.

6. Press the seam allowances toward the medium fabric and cut the strip set into six 1½" segments.

7. To assemble the alternate Chain blocks, lay out the segments from Steps 2, 4, and 6 for each block, as shown, and sew them together, referring to Matching and Pinning Tips on page 17. The directions of the seam allowances should alternate nicely because of the way you pressed each strip set.

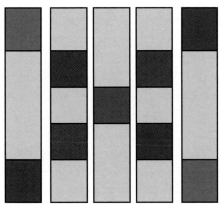

make 6 alternate Chain blocks

STRIP-PIECING THE SETTING TRIANGLES

Note: The same background fabric is featured in all of the setting triangles. Choose medium-to dark fabrics from the strips you have worked with previously.

1. From previously used strips, cut two 1½" x 16" medium strips and two 1½" x 16" background strips. Sew these strips together, alternating the colors as shown.

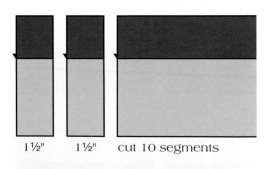

1½"   1½"   cut 10 segments

2. Press the seam allowances toward the medium fabrics and cut the strip set into ten 1½"-wide segments.

3. From more previously used strips, cut one 1½" x 16" medium strip and one 2½" x 16" background strip. Sew these strips into a strip set.

1½"   1½"   cut 10 segments

4. Press the seam allowance toward the medium fabric and cut the strip set into ten 1½"-wide segments.

5. From previously used strips, cut one 1½" x 16" background strip and one 1½" x 16" medium strip. Sew these strips into a strip set.

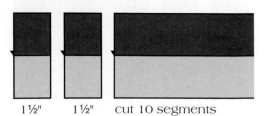

1½"   1½"   cut 10 segments

6. Press the seam allowance toward the medium fabric and cut the strip set into ten 1½"-wide segments.

7. Cut a 1½" x 42" medium strip into fourteen 1½" squares. You will need ten of these squares for the setting triangles and the four medium squares for the corner triangles.

8. Place the segments from Steps 2, 4, 6, and 7 in order for the setting triangles and sew them together, referring to Matching and Pinning Tips on page 17.

9. Lay an acrylic ruler along the diagonal edge of each of the setting triangles. Line up the ¼" marking on the ruler with the sewn corners on the setting triangles and mark a line there.

10. To prevent the bias edges from stretching the corner triangles out of shape, stay-stitch ⅛" inside the marked line, then rotary cut directly on the marked line.

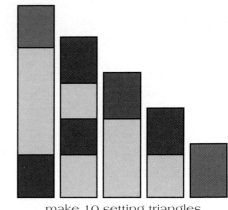

make 10 setting triangles

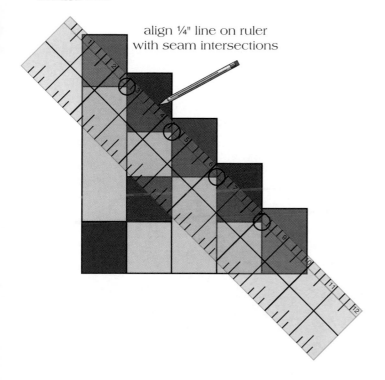

align ¼" line on ruler with seam intersections

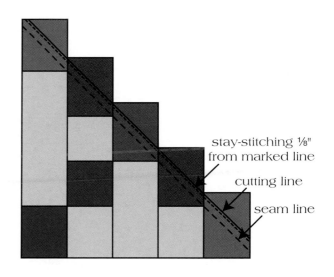

stay-stitching ⅛" from marked line

cutting line

seam line

STRIP-PIECING THE CORNER TRIANGLES

Note: The same background fabric is used throughout the corner triangles. Choose medium colors from previously used strips.

1. From previously used strips, cut two 1½" x 7" medium strips and one 1½" x 7" background strip. Sew the strips into a strip set.

2. Press the seam allowances toward the medium fabric and cut the strip set into four 1½"-wide segments.

3. To assemble the corner triangles, arrange the segments left over from strip-piecing the chain blocks, the segments from Step 2, and four 1½" medium squares left over from the setting triangles. Sew the three rows of

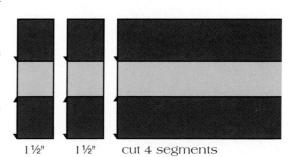

1½"   1½"   cut 4 segments

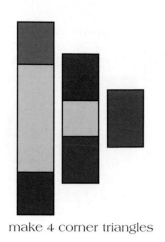

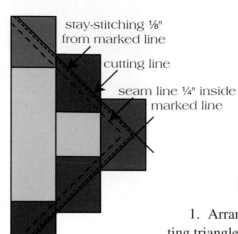

stay-stitching ⅛"
from marked line

cutting line

seam line ¼" inside
marked line

make 4 corner triangles

each corner triangle together, referring to "Matching and Pinning Tips" on page 17.

4. Mark, stay-stitch, and trim the edges of the corner triangles in the same manner as for the setting triangles, this time along both of the angled edges.

ASSEMBLING THE QUILT CENTER

1. Arrange the Ohio Star blocks, alternate Chain blocks, setting triangles, and corner triangles in diagonal rows.

2. Sew the diagonal rows together and add two corner squares at the opposite corners. Stitch very carefully to avoid stretching all of the bias edges out of shape.

Press the seam allowances very carefully; the stay-stitching should help to prevent distortions.

assembling the quilt center

ADDING THE BORDERS

1. Measure your quilt top vertically through the center to determine the correct length for the side inner border strips. Cut two 1½"-wide medium gold strips to this length and sew them to the sides of your quilt top, referring to the quilt diagram and to Straight Borders on page 26.

2. Measure your quilt top horizontally through the center to determine thc correct length for the top and bottom inner border strips. Cut two 1½"-wide medium gold strips to this length and sew them to the top and bottom edges of your quilt top, again referring to the quilt diagram and to Straight Borders.

3. Measure your quilt top vertically through the center to determine the correct length for the side outer border strips. Cut two 3"-wide dark blue strips to this length and sew them to the sides of your quilt top, using the quilt diagram and Straight Borders for reference.

4. Measure your quilt top horizontally through the center to determine the correct length for the top and bottom outer border strips. Cut two 3"-wide dark blue strips to this length and sew them to the top and bottom edges of your quilt top in the same manner as the other borders.

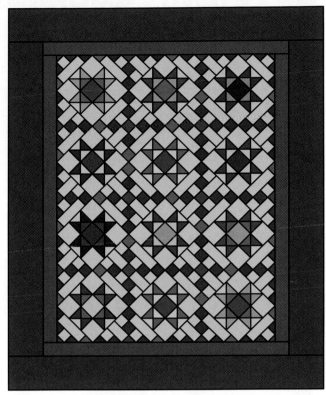

SCRAPPY STARS quilt diagram

QUILTING AND FINISHING

1. Press your finished quilt top and mark quilting designs, as desired, referring to Marking Methods on page 30.

2. Prepare the quilt sandwich for quilting, referring to Preparing the Backing on page 29, Layering and Basting on page 31.

3. Quilt by hand or machine, as desired, referring to Hand Quilting on page 31, or Machine Quilting on page 33. I quilted in the ditch around the design of the blocks with a free-motion leafy vine design around the outside border.

4. Bind the edges of the quilt and add a hanging sleeve, if desired, referring to Binding on page 33 and Attaching a Hanging Sleeve on page 35.

FRIENDS AMONG THE STARS

I used squares from my 2" scrap bin to make this wall quilt. This quilt is a great project for using up lots of squares in a wide range of colors.

FABRICS AND SUPPLIES

Note: If you are using pre-cut pieces from your scrap bins, refer to the Cutting List below for the number and type of pieces to cut for this project.

⅜" yard	assorted dark fabrics for Eight-Pointed Star blocks
⅜" yard	assorted dark fabrics for Friendship Stars in sashings
⅜" yard	assorted dark fabrics for sawtooth border
2 yards	light fabric for background and binding
1¼ yards	of fabric for backing
43" x 43"	piece of batting

CUTTING LIST

EIGHT-POINTED STAR BLOCKS

FROM THE DARK FABRIC:

Cut 36 squares	each 2" x 2" squares for block centers.
Cut 72 squares	each 2" x 2" for star points.

FROM THE LIGHT FABRIC:

Cut 36 rectangles	each 2" x 3½" for sides of blocks.
Cut 36 squares	each 2" x 2" for block corners.

FRIENDSHIP STAR BLOCKS AND SASHINGS

FROM THE DARK FABRIC:

Cut 48 squares	each 2" x 2" for star points.
Cut 8 squares	each 2⅜" x 2⅜" for outer star points.
Cut 16 squares	each 2" x 2" for star centers.

FROM THE LIGHT FABRIC:

Cut 4 squares	each 2" x 2" for sashing corners.
Cut 8 squares	each 2⅜" x 2⅜" for outer star points.
Cut 24 rectangles	each 2" x 6½" for sashings.

INNER BORDER

FROM THE LIGHT FABRIC:

Cut 2 strips	each 2" x 27½".
Cut 2 strips	each 2" x 30½".

SAWTOOTH BORDER

FROM THE DARK FABRIC:

Cut 40 squares	each 2⅜" x 2⅜".

FROM THE LIGHT FABRIC:

Cut 40 squares	each 2⅜" x 2⅜".

OUTER BORDER AND BINDING

FROM THE LIGHT FABRIC:

Cut 4 strips	each 3½" x 30½".
Cut 4 strips	each 2⅝" x 42" for binding.

CORNER FRIENDSHIP STARS

FROM THE DARK FABRIC:

Cut 12 squares	each 2" x 2".
Cut 4 squares	each 2⅜" x 2⅜".

FROM THE LIGHT FABRIC:

Cut 8 rectangles	each 2" x 3½".
Cut 4 squares	each 2⅜" x 2⅜".
Cut 4 squares	each 2" x 2" for border corners.

FINISHED QUILT	39" x 39"	*FINISHED BLOCK SIZE*	6" square

PIECING THE EIGHT-POINTED STAR BLOCKS

1. Draw a diagonal line from corner to corner on 72 of the 2" x 2" dark squares.

2. Place 2" x 2" dark square on top of a 2" x 3½" light rectangle, with the right sides together. Sew on the marked diagonal line. Trim the fabric ¼" from the seam line, open the fabrics, and press the seam toward the darker fabric.

3. Place a 2" x 2" dark square at the remaining end of the 2" x 3½" rectangle. Sew on the marked diagonal line, trim the seam to a ¼" seam allowance, and press the seam toward the darker fabric, as before. Make a total of 36 of these units.

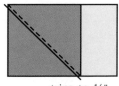

trim to ¼"

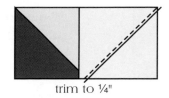
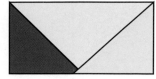
trim to ¼"   make 36

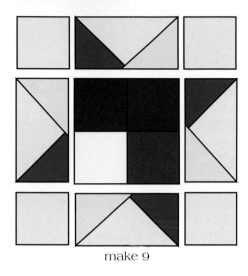

make 9

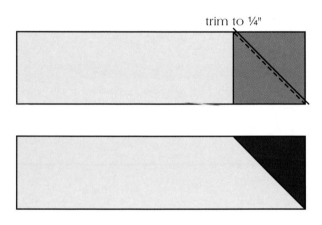

make 9

4. Lay out 4 different 2" dark squares for the center of each Eight-Pointed Star block. Chain-piece the squares together, referring to Chain Piecing on page 21. Make 9 of these units.

5. Lay out four units from Step 3, one unit from Step 4, and four 2" x 2" light squares for each Eight-Pointed Star block. Chain-piece the block together, referring to Chain-Piecing Blocks on page 22. Make 9 Eight-Pointed Star blocks.

PIECING THE FRIENDSHIP STARS AND SASHINGS

1. Referring to Quick Corner Triangles on page 18, draw a diagonal line from corner to corner on 48 of the 2" x 2" dark squares. Place a 2" dark square at one end of a 2" x 6½" light rectangle with right sides together. Sew on the marked diagonal line and trim the fabric, leaving a ¼" seam allowance. Press the seam allowance toward the darker fabric.

2. Place another 2" x 2" dark square at the remaining end of the 2" x 6½" light rectangle with right sides together. Sew on the diagonal line, trim the seam allowance to ¼", and press the seam allowance toward the darker fabric. Make 24 of these sashing units.

trim to ¼"

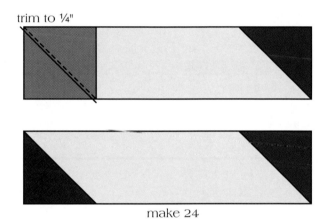

trim to ¼"

make 24

trim

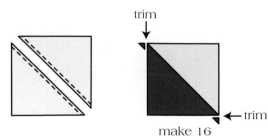

← trim

make 16

3. Referring to 2-in-1 Half-Square Triangle Units on page 19, place 8 of the 2⅜" x 2⅜" light squares on top of 8 of the 2⅜" x 2⅜" dark squares, with right sides together. Draw a diagonal line from corner to corner on the light squares, and sew ¼" from the marked line on both sides.

4. Rotary cut exactly on the marked diagonal line, separating the unit into two half-square triangle units. Press the seam allowances toward the darker fabric. Trim the excess fabric at the corners. Make a total of 16 of these half-square triangle units.

ASSEMBLING THE QUILT CENTER

1. Lay out the 9 Eight-Pointed Star blocks, the 24 sashing units, the 16 half-square triangle units, sixteen 2" x 2" dark squares, and four 2" x 2" light squares. Referring to Chain-Piecing Blocks on page 22, sew the units together into vertical rows as shown. Then sew the vertical rows together, completing the quilt center.

2. Sew a 2" x 27½" light inner border strip to the sides of the assembled quilt center and press the seam allowances toward the border strips. Sew a 2" x 30½" light inner border strip to the top and bottom edges of the assembled quilt center and press the seam allowances toward the border strips.

ADDING THE BORDERS

1. Referring to 2-in-1 Half-Square Triangle Units on page 19, draw a diagonal line corner to corner on forty 2⅜" light squares. Place the forty 2⅜" x 2⅜" light squares on top of forty 2⅜" x 2⅜" dark squares with right sides together. Sew a ¼" seam on both sides of the line and rotary cut the units apart on the marked diagonal lines. Trim the excess fabric in the seam allowance at the corners of each unit. Press the seam allowances toward the darker fabric. Make a total of 80 of these half-square triangle units.

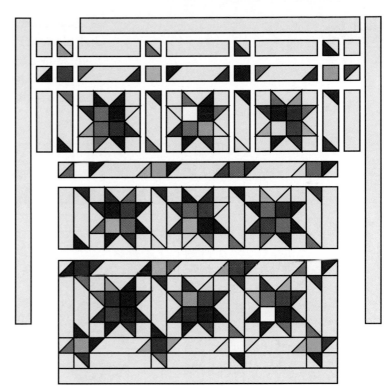

assembling the quilt center and inner border

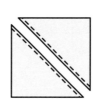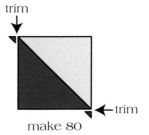

trim

make 80

trim

2. Arrange 20 half-square triangle units so that each group of 10 faces toward the center of the sawtooth border strip. Sew the half-square triangle units together in a row to create a sawtooth border. Make a total of 4 of these sawtooth border strips.

make 4

3. Sew a sawtooth border strip to each side of the quilt center as shown and press the seam allowances toward the borders strips. Sew a 2" x 2" light square to both ends of the two remaining sawtooth border strips and sew these border strips to the top and bottom edges of the quilt center. Press the seam allowances toward the border strips.

adding the Sawtooth and Friendship borders

trim to ¼"

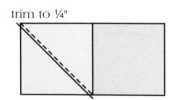

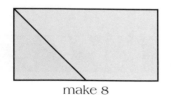

make 8

4. Draw a diagonal line corner to corner on a 2" x 2" dark square and place it at the end of a 2" x 3½" light rectangle. Sew on the marked diagonal line, trim the seam allowance to ¼", and press the seam allowance toward the dark fabric. Repeat to make a total of 8 of these Friendship Star point units.

5. Referring to Step 1 above, draw a diagonal line on four 2⅜" x 2⅜" light squares and place them on top of four 2⅜" x 2⅜" dark squares with right sides together. Sew a ¼" seam on both sides of the marked diagonal lines. Rotary cut the units apart on the marked diagonal lines and press the seam allowances toward the darker fabrics. Trim the excess fabric from the seam allowances at the corners. Make 8 of these half-square triangle units.

make 4

6. Sew together a Step 4 unit, a half-square triangle unit from Step 5, and a 2" x 2" dark square as shown. Make 4 of these Friendship Star corner units.

7. Sew a half-square triangle unit to a 2" x 2" light square. Make a total of 4 of these units.

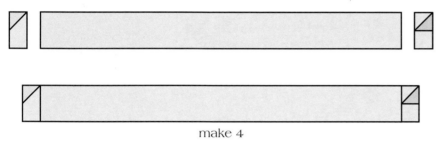

make 4

8. Sew a Step 4 unit to the left end of a 3½" x 30½" light border strip. Sew a Step 7 unit to the right end of the same border strip. Make 4 of these border units.

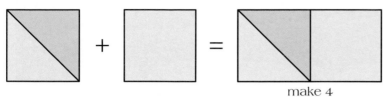

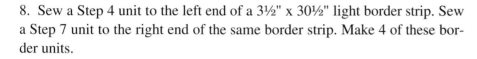

make 4

9. Referring to the quilt diagram, sew two Step 8 border units to the sides of the quilt center and press the seam allowances toward the borders. Sew a Step 6 corner unit to each end of the remaining two Step 8 border units. Sew these units to the top and bottom edges of the quilt center and press the seam allowances toward the outer borders.

QUILTING AND FINISHING

1. Press your finished quilt top and mark quilting designs as desired, referring to Marking Methods on page 30.

2. Prepare the quilt sandwich for quilting, referring to Preparing the Backing on page 29, Layering and Basting on page 31.

3. Quilt by hand or machine as desired, referring to Hand Quilting on page 31, or Machine Quilting on page 33. I quilted in the ditch in all the Friendship stars and Sawtooth borders, a simple cable for the inner border, and a pattern of tilting leaves in the outer border.

4. Bind the edges of the quilt and add a hanging sleeve, if desired, referring to Binding on page 33 and Attaching a Hanging Sleeve on page 35.

You can get creative with the centers of the Eight-Pointed Star blocks. Think about creating a checkerboard effect by the way you place lights and darks in the Four-Patches, or simply cut plain 3½" squares as a quick-piecing alternative to Four-Patches.

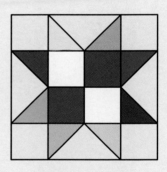

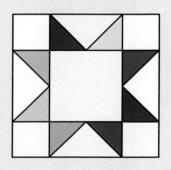

PASTEL PINWHEELS

As the saying goes, great minds think alike! I live in Michigan and my friend Kitty Sorgen lives in California – yet we both came up with the very same quilt design for a Pinwheel block quilt. This is my version; you can see Kitty's, EL NIÑO, WIND, WATER, AND MUD, on page 124. At the end of the project instructions, you will also find Size and Cutting Charts for twin, double/queen, and king-sized quilts, so you can make Pinwheel quilts in other sizes.

FABRICS AND SUPPLIES

Note: If you are using pre-cut pieces from your scrap bins, refer to the Cutting List for the number and type of pieces to cut for this project. If you are making this quilt in another size, refer to the charts on page 54 for Quilt Size, Fabrics and Supplies, and Cutting List.

¾ yard	assorted pastel fabrics for Pinwheel blocks
1¾ yards	light background fabric for Pinwheel blocks and alternate plain blocks
¾ yard	mint green fabric for inner border
⅞ yard	medium purple fabric for outer border and binding
1⅝ yards	of fabric for backing
43" x 55"	piece of batting

FINISHED QUILT	39" x 51"
FINISHED BLOCK SIZE	9" square

CUTTING LIST

Note: Two 2⅜" x 2⅜" light squares and two 2⅜" x 2⅜" dark squares will make one small Pinwheel unit.

FROM THE ASSORTED PASTEL FABRICS:

Cut 84 squares	each 2⅜" x 2⅜" for small Pinwheel units.
Cut 8 squares	each 2⅞" x 2⅞" for large Pinwheel units.

FROM THE LIGHT BACKGROUND FABRIC:

Cut 84 squares	each 2⅜" x 2⅜" for small Pinwheel units.
Cut 8 squares	each 2⅞" x 2⅞" for large Pinwheel units.
Cut 24 squares	each 3½" x 3½" for plain squares.
Cut 17 strips	each 3½" x 9½" for sashings.

FROM THE MINT GREEN FABRIC:

Cut 4 strips	each 4½" x 42" for inner border.

FROM THE MEDIUM PURPLE FABRIC:

Cut 6 strips	each 2½" x 42" for outer border.
Cut 5 strips	each 2⅝" x 42" for binding.

PIECING THE SMALL PINWHEEL UNITS

1. Referring to 2-in-1 Half-Square Triangle Units on page 19, draw a diagonal line on each of the eighty-four 2⅜" light squares. Place these light squares on top of the eighty-four 2⅜" x 2⅜" pastel squares, with right sides together. Take care to choose 2 same-color pastel squares so that you will end up with 4 matching half-square triangle units for each small Pinwheel unit.

2. Sew a ¼" seam on each side of the marked diagonal lines. Rotary cut the units apart on the diagonal lines and press the seam allowances toward the pastel fabrics. Trim the excess fabric from the seam allowances at the corners of the units. Make sure that you have 4 matching half-square triangle units in each pastel fabric and a total of 168 half-square triangle units.

3. Lay out 4 half-square triangle units for each of the 42 small Pinwheel units, and sew them together, referring to Chain Piecing on page 21. As you do this, press each seam allowance open rather than to one side, so the finished units will lie flatter.

Refer to the chart on page 54 for the number of small Pinwheel units needed for other quilt sizes.

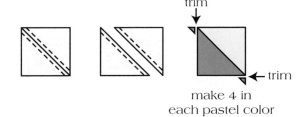

make 4 in each pastel color

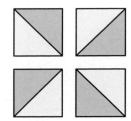

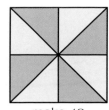

make 42

Refer to the chart on page 54 for the number of Pinwheel blocks needed for your size quilt.

4. Arrange 5 small Pinwheel units and four 3½" x 3½" light background squares in position for a Nine-patch block. Referring to Chain-Piecing Blocks on page 22, sew these units together to create the Pinwheel block.

5. Lay out the 6 Pinwheel blocks, the seventeen 3½" x 9½" light strips, and 12 small Pinwheel units and sew them together, referring to Chain-Piecing Blocks on page 22.

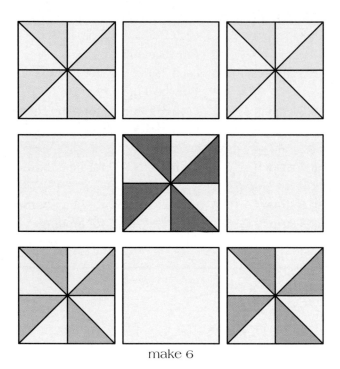

make 6

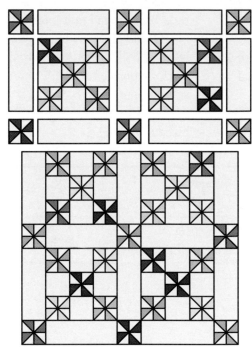

assembling the quilt center

PIECING THE PINWHEEL CORNER BLOCKS

1. Mark a diagonal line from corner to corner on eight 2⅞" x 2⅞" light squares. Place these light squares on top of eight 2⅞" x 2⅞" pastel squares, with right sides together.

2 Referring to Steps 2 and 3 on page 51, piece the Pinwheel corner blocks in the same manner as for the small Pinwheel units.

ADDING THE BORDERS

1. Measure your quilt top vertically through the center, to determine the correct length for the 4½"-wide side border strips. Cut two 4½"-wide mint green strips to this length. Measure your quilt top horizontally through the center to determine the correct length for the 4½"-wide top and bottom border strips. Cut two 4½"-wide mint green strips to this length.

2. Sew the two 4½"-wide mint green border strips to the sides of the quilt center, referring to Straight Borders on page 26. Press the seam allowances toward the border strips.

3. Referring to the quilt diagram at right, sew a large Pinwheel corner block to each end of the top and bottom border strips. Press these seam allowances toward the border strips. Sew the two 4½"-wide mint green border strips with the large Pinwheel units attached to the top and bottom edges of the quilt center, referring to the previous diagram and to Straight Borders on page 26. Press the seam allowances toward the border strips.

4. Measure your quilt top vertically through the center to determine the correct length for the 2½"-wide side outer border strips. Sew together two 2½"-wide medium purple strips for each of the side borders and trim the sewn strips to this length. Sew the two 2½"-wide medium purple outer border strips to the sides of the quilt center, referring to the previous diagram and to Straight Borders on page 26. Press the seam allowances toward the border strips.

5. Measure your quilt top horizontally through the center, to determine the correct length for the 2½" wide top and bottom outer border strips. Cut two 2½" wide medium purple strips to this length. Sew the 2½"-wide medium purple outer border strips to the top and bottom edges of the quilt center, referring to the previous diagram and to Straight Borders on page 26. Press the seam allowances toward the border strips.

adding the borders

QUILTING AND FINISHING

1. Press your finished quilt top and mark quilting designs, as desired, referring to Marking Methods on page 30.

2. Prepare the quilt sandwich for quilting, referring to Preparing the Backing on page 29, Layering and Basting on page 31.

3. Quilt by hand or machine, as desired, referring to Hand Quilting on page 31, or Machine Quilting on page 33. I quilted diagonal lines through the center of the quilt, following the diagonal lines of the small Pinwheel units. In the mint green border, I quilted a heart design and did not quilt any design in the medium purple border.

4. Bind the edges of the quilt and add a hanging sleeve, if desired, referring to Binding on page 33, and Attaching a Hanging Sleeve on page 35.

UNITS AND BLOCKS

	Pinwheel Units in Nine-Patch Pinwheel Blocks
Twin	120
Full/Queen	210
King	245

	Nine-Patch Pinwheel Blocks
Twin	24 (4 across; 6 down)
Full/Queen	42 (6 across; 7 down)
King	49 (7 across; 7 down)

	Pinwheel Units in Sashings
Twin	35
Full/Queen	56
King	64

	Large Corner Pinwheel Units
Twin	4
Full/Queen	4
King	4

	3½" x 3½" Plain Blocks
Twin	96
Full/Q	168
King	196

QUILT SIZES

Twin	63" x 87"
Full/Queen	87" x 99"
King	99" x 99"

FABRICS AND SUPPLIES

	Darks	*Light Background*	*Inner Border*	*Outer Border*
Twin	1⅝ yards	3¾ yards	1¼ yards	¾ yard
Full/Queen	2¾ yards	6 yards	1½ yards	⅞ yard
King	3 yards	7 yards	1½ yards	1 yard

	Backing	*Batting*	*Binding*
Twin	67" x 91"	71" x 95"	¾ yard
Full/Queen	91" x 103"	95" x 107"	⅞ yard
King	103" x 103"	107" x 107"	1 yard

CUTTING LIST

	2⅜" pastel squares	*2⅜" light squares*	*3½" x 9½" light strips*	*3½" light squares*
Twin	310	310	58	96
Full/Queen	532	532	97	168
King	618	618	112	196

	2⅞" pastel squares	*2⅞" light squares*	*4½" x 42" inner border strips*	*2½" x 42½" outer border strips*
Twin	8	8	7	8
Full/Queen	8	8	9	10
King	8	8	9	12

	Batting	*2⅝" x 42" binding strips*
Twin	67" x 91"	8
Full/Queen	91" x 103"	10
King	103" x 103"	10

LEAH'S GARDEN PATH

Myrtice Clouse's quilt, LEAH'S GARDEN PATH, features the Pinwheels All Around pattern, which is one of my all-time favorites. This is a perfect project for using up those 2" squares that can accumulate so quickly in your scrap bins. The Pinwheel blocks produce an interesting diagonal pattern that breaks up the squares visually and produces a feeling of movement throughout the quilt.

FABRICS AND SUPPLIES

Note: If you are using pre-cut pieces from your scrap bins, refer to the Cutting List for the number and type of pieces to cut for this project. If you are making this quilt in another size, refer to the charts on page 61 for Quilt Sizes, Fabrics and Supplies, and Cutting Lists.

½ yard	each of 8 different light fabrics for Checkerboard blocks
½ yard	each of 8 different dark fabrics for Checkerboard blocks
⅞ yard	each of 4 different light fabrics for Pinwheel blocks
⅞ yard	each of 4 different dark fabrics for Pinwheel blocks
1⅜ yards	red fabric for inner border
2⅜ yards	dark blue fabric for outer border and binding
106" x 106"	piece of batting

FINISHED QUILT	102" x 102"
FINISHED BLOCK SIZE	6" square

CUTTING LIST

FROM EACH OF THE 8 LIGHT FABRICS:

Cut 5 strips	each 2" x 42" for Checkerboard blocks. You should have a total of 40 light strips.

FROM EACH OF THE 8 DARK FABRICS:

Cut 5 strips	each 2" x 42" for Checkerboard blocks. You should have a total of 40 dark strips.

FROM EACH OF THE 4 LIGHT FABRICS:

Cut 258 squares	each 3⅞" x 3⅞" for Pinwheel blocks.

FROM EACH OF THE 4 DARK FABRICS:

Cut 258 squares	each 3⅞" x 3⅞" for Pinwheel blocks.

FROM THE RED FABRIC:

Cut 12 strips	each 3½" x 42" for inner border.

FROM THE DARK BLUE FABRIC:

Cut 12 strips	each 3½" x 42" for outer border.
Cut 10 strips	each 2⅝" x 42" for binding.

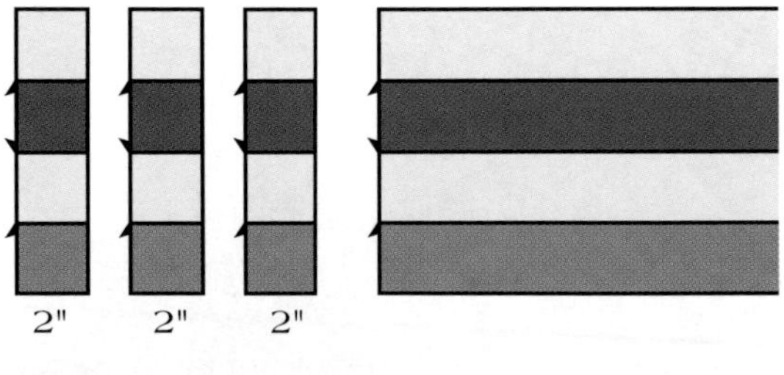

2"   2"   2"

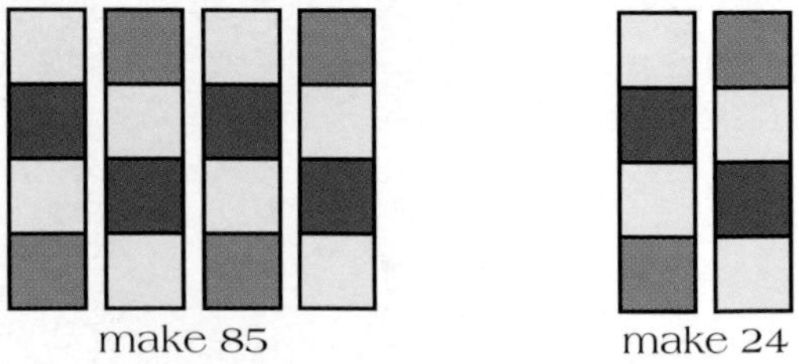

make 85   make 24

PIECING THE CHECKERBOARD BLOCKS

1. Sew the 2" x 42" light strips and the 2" x 42" dark strips into 20 strip sets, each containing 2 dark and 2 light strips, alternating the colors as shown. Press the seam allowances toward the dark fabrics. Rotary cut the strip sets into 2"-wide segments.

2. Arrange 4 segments from Step 1, alternating the dark and light colors, as shown. Sew the strips together, matching the intersections, to complete a Checkerboard block. Make a total of 85 Checkerboard blocks.

PIECING THE HALF- AND QUARTER-CHECKERBOARD BLOCKS

1. Sew two 2"-wide segments together, alternating colors as shown, to create a Half-Checkerboard block. Make a total of 24 Half-Checkerboard blocks.

2. Remove the stitching between the middle strips on eight 2"-wide segments. Rearrange the half-segments and sew them together, as shown, to create a Quarter-Checkerboard block. Make a total of 8 Quarter-Checkerboard blocks.

make 8

PIECING THE PINWHEEL AND HALF-PINWHEEL BLOCKS

1. Draw a diagonal line from corner to corner on each of the 3⅞" x 3⅞" light squares. Place a 3⅞" x 3⅞" light on top of a dark square, with right sides together. Sew a ¼" seam on both sides of the marked line, referring to 2-in-1 Half-Square Triangle Units on page 19.

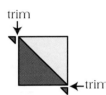

trim

←trim

2. Rotary cut on the marked diagonal line, separating the units. Press the seam allowances toward the dark fabric, and trim the excess fabric at each end of the seams. You will need a total of 512 half-square triangle units.

3. Sew 4 half-square triangle units together to create a Pinwheel block, referring to Chain-Piecing Blocks on page 22. Make a total of 84 Pinwheel blocks.

4. Sew 2 half-square triangle units to create a Half-Pinwheel block. Make a total of 88 Half-Pinwheel blocks.

make 84   make 88

ASSEMBLING THE QUILT CENTER

Lay out 84 Pinwheel blocks, 28 Half-Pinwheel blocks, 85 Checkerboard blocks, 24 Half-Checkerboard blocks, and 4 Quarter-Checkerboard blocks as shown to create the quilt center. Referring to Chain-Piecing Blocks on page 22, sew the blocks and units together in vertical rows; then sew the vertical rows together to complete the quilt center.

ADDING THE INNER BORDER

1. Sew together three 3½" x 42" red strips. Repeat to make three more of these border strips.

2. Measure your quilt top vertically through the center to determine the correct length for the side inner borders. Trim two of the sewn border strips to this length and sew them to the sides of the quilt center, referring to the quilt diagram on page 58. Press the seam allowances toward the inner borders.

3. Measure your quilt top horizontally through the center to determine the correct length for the top and bottom inner borders. Trim the remaining two sewn border strips to this length. Referring to the quilt diagram on page 58, sew the trimmed border strips to the top and bottom edges of the quilt center. Press the seam allowances toward the inner borders.

Whenever you need to ease in a bit of extra length in a quilt seam, make it a practice to sew with the larger piece on the bottom. This will allow the feed dogs of your sewing machine to help you ease in the extra length evenly.

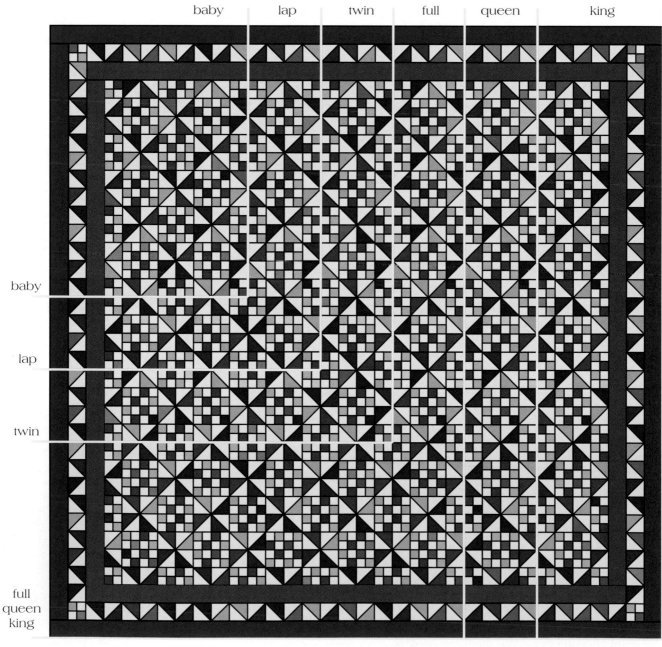

LEAH'S GARDEN quilt diagram

ADDING THE PIECED BORDER

1. Referring to the quilt diagram on page 58, sew together a row of Half-Pinwheel blocks. Make a total of 4 of these pieced borders.

2. Referring to the quilt diagram, sew a Quarter-Checkerboard block to each end of two of the pieced borders. Press each of the seam allowances in the same direction.

3. Referring to the quilt diagram, sew two of the pieced borders to the sides of the quilt center, keeping the seams of the pieced border lined up with the seams in the quilt center. Press the seam allowances toward the inner border.

4. Sew the two pieced borders with Quarter-Checkerboard blocks to the top and bottom edges of the quilt center, taking care to align the seams in the pieced borders with the seams in the quilt center as before. Press the seam allowances toward the inner border.

> If you need to make an adjustment for ease when you add the pieced middle border, check the seams between the Half-Pinwheel blocks. You can sew slightly wider (or narrower) seams in several different places along the border to almost invisibly ease in 1" or more of extra length.

ADDING THE OUTER BORDER

1. Sew together three 3½" x 42" dark blue strips. Repeat to make three more of these border strips.

2. Measure your quilt top vertically through the center to determine the correct length for the outer borders. Trim two of the sewn border strips to this length. Referring to the quilt diagram, sew them to the sides of the quilt center. Press the seam allowances toward the outer border.

3. Measure your quilt top horizontally through the center to determine the correct length for the top and bottom outer borders. Referring to the quilt diagram, sew the remaining two sewn border strips to the top and bottom edges of the quilt center. Press the seam allowances toward the outer border.

QUILTING AND FINISHING

1. Press your finished quilt top and mark quilting designs, as desired, referring to Marking Methods on page 30.

2. Prepare the quilt sandwich for quilting, referring to Preparing the Backing on page 29, Layering and Basting on page 31.

3. Quilt by hand or machine, as desired, referring to Hand Quilting on page 31, or Machine Quilting on page 33 I quilted in the ditch to make the different squares and lights and darks of the pinwheel design stand out. If you want the Checkerboard blocks to recede a bit, try quilting an overall pattern on each of these blocks.

4. Bind the edges of the quilt and add a hanging sleeve, if desired, referring to Binding on page 33 and Attaching a Hanging Sleeve on page 35.

CUTTING LIST

	2" x 42" LIGHT STRIPS FOR CHECKERBOARD BLOCKS	2" x 42" DARK STRIPS FOR CHECKERBOARD BLOCKS
Baby*	6	6
Lap	10	10
Twin	16	16
Full	28	28
Queen	34	34

*Note: For baby quilt size, if you cut your strips in half, you can utilize all 8 of your colors.

	3⅞" x 3⅞" LIGHT SQUARES FOR PINWHEEL BLOCKS	3⅞" x 3⅞" DARK SQUARES FOR PINWHEEL BLOCKS
Baby	48 (12 in each fabric)	48 (12 in each fabric)
Lap	80 (20 in each fabric)	80 (20 in each fabric)
Twin	120 (30 in each fabric)	120 (30 in each fabric)
Full	192 (48 in each fabric)	192 (48 in each fabric)
Queen	224 (56 in each fabric)	224 (56 in each fabric)

	3½" x 42" INNER BORDER STRIPS	3½" x 42" OUTER BORDER STRIPS
Baby	4	6
Lap	6	7
Twin	7	8
Full	8	10
Queen	10	12

	BATTING	2⅜" x 42" BINDING STRIPS
Baby	47" x 60"	5
Lap	60" x 70"	6
Twin	52" x 82"	8
Full	64" x 100"	9
Queen	94" x 106"	10

BLOCKS, HALF-BLOCKS, AND QUARTER-BLOCKS

	CHECKERBOARD BLOCKS	HALF-CHECKERBOARD BLOCKS	QUARTER-CHECKERBOARD BLOCKS
Baby	8	6	4
Lap	18	10	4
Twin	32	14	4
Full	59	20	4
Queen	72	22	4

	PINWHEEL BLOCKS	HALF-PINWHEEL BLOCKS
Baby	7	10
Lap	17	14
Twin	31	18
Full	58	24
Queen	71	26

	BORDER HALF-PINWHEEL BLOCKS	BORDER QUARTER-CHECKERBOARD BLOCKS
Baby	24	4
Lap	32	4
Twin	40	4
Full	52	4
Queen	56	4

QUILT SIZES

Baby	42" x 54"
Lap	54" x 66"
Twin	66" x 78"
Full	78" x 102"
Queen	90" x 102"

FABRICS AND SUPPLIES

	8 DIFFERENT LIGHTS FOR CHECKERBOARD BLOCKS	8 DIFFERENT DARKS FOR CHECKERBOARD BLOCKS	4 DIFFERENT LIGHTS FOR PINWHEEL BLOCKS	4 DIFFERENT DARKS FOR PINWHEEL BLOCKS
Baby	⅛ yard each	⅛ yard each	¼ yard each	¼ yard each
Lap	¼ yard each	¼ yard each	⅜ yard each	⅜ yard each
Twin	¼ yard each	¼ yard each	½ yard each	½ yard each
Full	⅜ yard each	⅜ yard each	⅔ yard each	⅔ yard each
Queen	⅜ yard each	⅜ yard each	⅞ yard each	⅞ yard each

	INNER BORDER	OUTER BORDER	BACKING	BINDING
Baby	½ yard	¾ yard	2½ yards	½ yard
Lap	¾ yard	⅞ yard	4 yards	⅝ yard
Twin	⅞ yard	1 yard	4¾ yards	¾ yard
Full	1 yard	1⅛ yards	6 yards	⅞ yard
Queen	1⅛ yards	1⅜ yards	6 yards	1 yard

ALWAYS A FARMER'S DAUGHTER

For this quilt, I wanted a color scheme that would accentuate the stars in the classic Farmer's Daughter blocks. I chose rich, dark reds, blues, browns, and golds for the stars and surrounded them with lighter tan and cream-colored background fabrics. The result is a scrappy design that sparkles with energy.

CUTTING LIST

FROM THE DARK FABRICS:

Cut 8 strips   each 2½" x 42" for Farmer's Daughter
                    blocks.
Cut 9 strips   each 2½" x 42".
    From these strips, cut 144 squares,
    each 2½" x 2½", for Farmer's Daughter blocks.
Note: If you are working with scraps, you will need 8
dark squares in the same fabric for the points and 5
dark squares of the same fabric for the block center in
each Farmer's Daughter block.

FROM THE CONTRAST FABRICS:

Cut 7 strips   each 2½" x 42" for Farmer's Daughter
                    blocks.
Note: If you are working with scraps, you will need 4
squares, each 2½" x 2½" in the same contrasting fabric
for each Farmer's Daughter block.

FROM THE LIGHT BACKGROUND FABRIC:

Cut 6 strips   each 2½" x 42".
    From these strips, cut 48 rectangles
    each 2½" x 6½" for Farmer's Daughter blocks.
    Cut 48 squares, each 2½" x 2½", for Farmer's Daugh-
                    ter blocks from the same strips.
Cut 3 strips   each 11¼" x 42".
    From these strips, cut 9 squares
    each 11¼" x 11¼" for Hourglass blocks.
Cut 6 strips   each 2¼" x 42".
    From these strips, cut 24 pieces
    using Template A for Border blocks.
    Cut 24 pieces   using Template A reversed for Border
                    blocks from the same strips.
Note: Alternate Template A and A reversed when you
cut these pieces.
Cut 2 strips   each 11¼" x 42".
    From these strips, cut 4 squares
    each 11¼" x 11¼" for Border blocks.
Cut 3 strips   each 2¼" x 42".
    From these strips, cut 12 rectangles
    each 2¼" x 4" for Corner blocks.
    Cut 4 pieces   using Template A and 4 pieces using
                    Template A reversed for Corner blocks
                    from the same strips.

FROM THE MEDIUM TAN BACKGROUND FABRIC:

Cut 4 strips   each 2½" x 42".
    From these strips, cut 24 rectangles,
    each 2½" x 6½", for Farmer's Daughter blocks.

Cut 2 strips   each 2½" x 42"
    From these strips, cut 24 squares,
    each 2½" x 2½", for Farmer's Daughter blocks.
Cut 6 strips   each 11¼" x 11¼".
    From these strips, cut 9 squares,
    each 11¼" x 11¼", for Hourglass blocks.
    Cut 9 squares   each 11¼" x 11¼" for Border blocks
                    from these same strips.
Cut 2 squares   each 5⅞" x 5⅞" for Corner blocks.
Cut 2 squares   each 6¼" x 6¼" for Corner blocks.

FROM THE MEDIUM RED FABRIC:

Cut 6 strips   each 2¼" x 42".
    From these strips, cut 24 pieces
    using Template A for Border blocks.
    Cut 24 pieces using Template A reversed for Border
                    blocks from the same strips.
Note: Alternate Template A and A reversed when you cut
these pieces.
Cut 4 pieces using Template B for Border blocks.
Cut 4 pieces using Template B for Corner blocks.

FROM THE DARK RED FABRIC:

Cut 10 strips   each 3½" x 42" for inner border.

FROM THE MEDIUM GREEN FABRIC:

Cut 3 strips   each 2¼" x 42".
    From these strips, cut 48 squares,
    each 2¼" x 2¼", for Border blocks.
Cut 3 strips   each 6¼" x 42".
    From these strips, cut 12 squares,
    each 6¼" x 6¼", for Border blocks.
    Cut 2 squares   each 6¼" x 6¼" for Corner blocks from
                    the same strips.
Cut 4 squares   each 4" x 4" for Corner blocks.

FROM THE DARK GREEN FABRIC:

Cut 10 strips   each 4½" x 42" for outer border.
Cut 10 strips   each 2⅝" x 42" for binding.

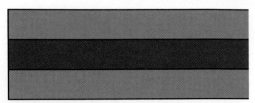

make 2 strip sets

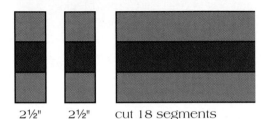

2½"   2½"   cut 18 segments

make 3 strip sets

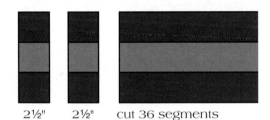

2½"   2½"   cut 36 segments

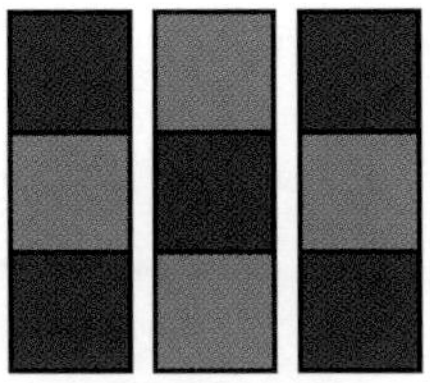

make 18

FABRICS AND SUPPLIES

Note: If you are using pre-cut pieces from your scrap bins, refer to the Cutting List on page 63 for the number and type of pieces to cut for this project. If you are making this quilt in the other size, refer to the charts on page 70 for Quilt Size, Fabrics and Supplies, and Cutting List.

1⅜ yards	dark fabrics for Farmer's Daughter blocks
⅞ yard	contrast fabrics for Farmer's Daughter blocks
2¾ yards	light background fabric for Farmer's Daughter, hourglass, border, and corner blocks
2¾ yards	medium tan background fabric for Farmer's Daughter, hourglass, border, and corner blocks
¾ yard	medium red fabric for border and corner blocks
1⅛ yards	dark red fabric for inner border
1 yard	medium green fabric for border and corner blocks
2⅛ yards	dark green fabric for outer border and binding
87" x 107"	piece of batting

FINISHED QUILT	84" x 104"
FINISHED BLOCK SIZE	10"

PIECING THE FARMER'S DAUGHTER BLOCKS

1. Sew two 2½" x 42" contrast strips and one 2½" x 42" dark strip into a strip set. Make 2 of these strip sets. Press the seam allowances toward the dark fabric. Rotary cut the strip sets into a total of 18 segments, each 2½" wide.

2. Sew two 2½" x 42" dark strips and one 2½" x 42" contrast strip into a strip set. Make 3 of these strip sets. Press the seam allowances toward the dark fabric. Rotary cut the strip sets into 36 segments, each 2½" wide.

3. Arrange a segment from Step 1 and two segments from Step 2 in configuration for the center of the Farmer's Daughter block. Sew the segments together, matching the intersections. Press the seam allowances toward the middle segment. Make 18 of these block centers.

4. Draw a diagonal line from corner to corner on 8 of the 2½" x 2½" dark squares. Place one of these squares at the left end of a 2½" x 6½" light rectangle. Sew on the marked diagonal line. Trim the seam allowance to ¼" from the seam line. Press the seam allowance toward the dark fabric.

5. Place another 2½" x 2½" dark square at the other end of the same 2½" x 6½" light rectangle. Sew on the marked diagonal line. Trim the seam allowance to ¼" from the seam line. Press the seam allowance toward the dark fabric. Make a total of 48 of these units using the light background fabric and the same-color dark fabric for 12 of the Farmer's Daughter blocks. For the remaining 6 Farmer's Daughter blocks, make a total of 24 of these units using the medium tan background fabric and the same-color dark fabric for each block.

make 48   make 24

6. Lay out the 4 units from Step 5, four 2½" x 2½" light background squares, and a matching block center in configuration for a Farmer's Daughter block. Referring to Chain-Piecing Blocks on page 22, sew the units together into three vertical rows; then sew the vertical rows together to complete the block. Make a total of 12 Farmer's Daughter blocks using the light background fabric and same-color dark fabrics in each block. Make a total of 6 Farmer's Daughter blocks using the medium tan background fabric and same-color dark fabrics in each block.

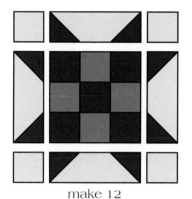

make 12

make 6

PIECING THE HOURGLASS BLOCKS

1. Draw a diagonal line from corner to corner in both directions on each of the light 11¼" x 11¼" light background squares.

2. Place a marked 11¼" x 11¼" light background square on top of an 11¼" x 11¼" medium tan background square, with right sides together. Sew a ¼" seam on both sides of one diagonal line.

3. Rotary cut on the marked diagonal line between the seam lines, creating 2 half-square triangle units. Press the seam allowances toward the medium tan fabric and trim the excess fabric at both ends of the seam allowances. Make a total of 34 of these half-square triangle units.

4. Place 2 half-square units right sides together, with the light and medium triangles facing in opposite directions. Extend the drawn line from the light triangle across the medium triangle and sew a ¼" seam on both sides of this marked line.

5. Rotary cut on the diagonal line between the seam lines. Press the seam allowances to one side. Trim the excess fabric at both ends of the seam allowances. Make a total of 17 hourglass blocks.

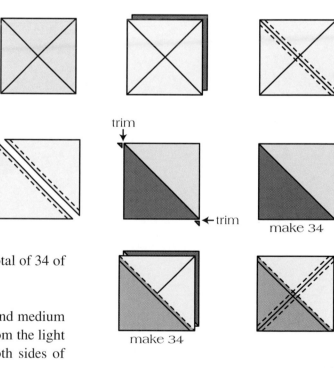

trim

trim

make 34

make 34

trim

trim

make 17

PIECING THE BORDER BLOCKS

1. Rotary cut the remaining 11¼" x 11¼" light background squares and the remaining 11¼" x 11¼" medium tan squares from corner to corner in both directions for a total of 4 triangles each. In the same manner, rotary cut the 6¼" x 6¼" medium green squares from corner to corner in both directions, for total of 4 triangles each. You will need a total of 14 light triangles and 34 medium tan triangles.

2. Place a 2¼" x 2¼" medium green square right sides together with a medium red piece cut from template A and sew the pieces together along the squared-off edge. Press the seam allowance toward the medium green square. Make 24 of these units. In the same manner, place a 2¼" x 2¼" medium green square right sides together with a medium red piece cut from template A reversed and sew the pieces together along the squared-off edge. Press the seam allowance toward the medium green square. Make 24 of these units.

3. Place a light background piece cut from Template A right sides together with a medium green triangle, and sew them together as shown. Press the seam allowance toward the medium green triangle. Make 24 of these units. In the same manner, place a light background piece cut from Template A reversed right sides together with a medium green triangle and sew them together as shown. Press the seam allowance toward the medium green triangle. Make 24 of these units.

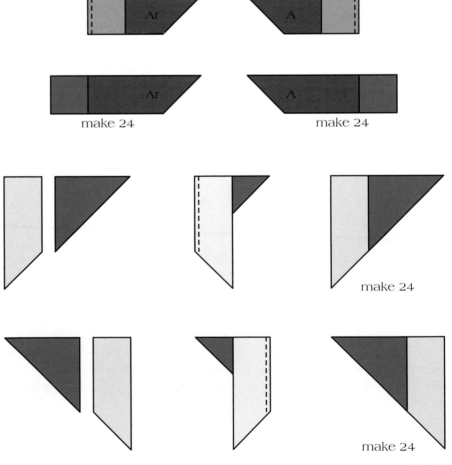

make 24   make 24

make 24

make 24

4. Place a Step 2 unit with the A piece on top of a Step 3 unit, with right sides together, and the seam allowances pressed in opposite directions. Sew the units together as shown. Press the seam allowance toward the Step 2 unit. Make 24 of these units. In the same manner, place a Step 2 unit with the A reversed piece on top of a Step 3 unit, with right sides together, and the seam allowances pressed in opposite directions. Sew the units together as shown. Press the seam allowance toward the Step 2 unit. Make 24 of these units.

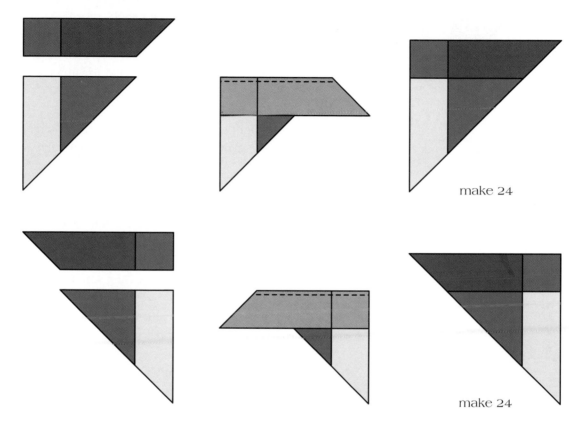

make 24

make 24

5. Lay out the triangle units from Step 4 and a light background triangle and a medium tan background triangle in configuration for a border block. Sew the medium tan triangle to a Step 4 unit and press the seam allowance toward the medium tan triangle. Sew the light background triangle to the remaining Step 4 unit and press the seam allowance toward the light triangle. Sew the two units together to complete the border block, and press the seam allowance to one side. Make a total of 14 of these border blocks.

6. Repeat Step 5 to make a total of 10 border blocks using 2 medium tan background triangles each.

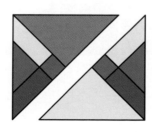

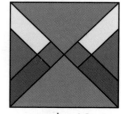

make 14   make 10

make 4

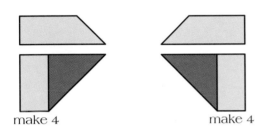

make 4   make 4

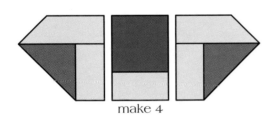

make 4   make 4

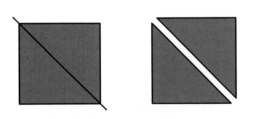

make 4

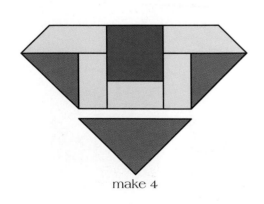

make 4

PIECING THE CORNER BLOCKS

1. Sew a 4" x 4" medium green square to a 2¼" x 4" light background rectangle. Press the seam allowance toward the medium green square. Make 4 of these units.

2. Rotary cut the two 6¼" x 6¼" medium tan background squares and the two 6¼" x 6¼" square medium green squares from corner to corner in both directions, for a total of 8 triangles each.

3. Sew a 2¼" x 4" light rectangle to one side of a medium tan background triangle. Press the seam allowance toward the light rectangle. Make 4 of these units.

4. Sew a 2¼" x 4" light rectangle to the other side of a medium tan background triangle. Press the seam allowance toward the light rectangle. Make 4 of these units.

5. Sew a light background piece cut from Template A to a Step 3 unit. Press the seam allowance toward the Step 3 unit. Make 4 of these units.

6. Sew a light background piece cut from Template A reversed to a Step 4 unit. Press the seam allowance toward the Step 4 unit. Make 4 of these units.

7. Sew a Step 5 unit and a Step 6 unit to the sides of a Step 1 unit. Press the seam allowances toward the Step 1 unit. Make 4 of these units.

8. Rotary cut the two 5⅞" medium tan squares in half from corner to corner, for a total of 4 triangles.

9. Sew a Step 8 medium tan triangle to a Step 7 unit. Press the seam allowance toward the medium tan triangle Make 4 of these units.

10. Sew a medium green triangle to each side of a medium red piece cut from Template B. Press the seam allowance toward the medium green triangle. Make 4 of these units. Sew one of these units to a Step 9 unit to complete a corner block. Press the seam allowance to one side. Make 4 of these corner blocks.

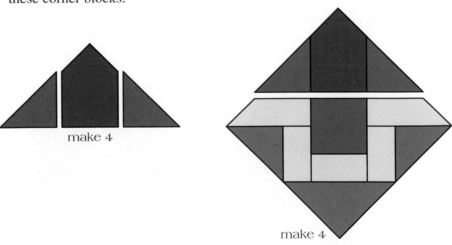

make 4

make 4

ASSEMBLING THE QUILT CENTER

1. Arrange the 18 Farmer's Daughter blocks, the 17 Hourglass blocks, the 24 border blocks, and the 4 corner blocks in configuration for the quilt center.

2. Referring to "Chain-Piecing Blocks" on page 22 and the quilt diagram below, sew the blocks together into 7 vertical rows. Press the seam allowances between blocks in the same direction within each row and in opposite directions in alternating rows. Then sew the vertical rows together, matching intersections to complete the quilt center. Press the seam allowances between rows in the same direction.

ADDING THE BORDERS

1. Sew the short ends of two 3½" x 42" dark red inner border strips. Make 2 of these border strips for the top and bottom inner borders. Sew together three 3½" x 42" dark red inner border strips. Make 2 of these border strips for the side inner borders. Press the seam allowances open.

2. Measure your quilt top vertically through the center to determine the correct length for the side inner borders. Cut two 3½"-wide dark red border strips to this length and sew them to the sides of your quilt top. Press the seam allowances toward the dark red borders.

3. Measure your quilt top horizontally through the center to determine the correct length for the top and bottom inner borders. Cut two 3½"-wide dark

ALWAYS A FARMER'S DAUGHTER quilt diagram

red border strips to this length and sew them to the top and bottom edges of your quilt top, referring to the quilt diagram on page 69. Press the seam allowances toward the dark red borders.

4. Sew together three 4½"-wide dark green border strips and press the seam allowances open. Repeat to make another border strip like this. Measure your quilt top vertically through the center to determine the correct length for the side outer borders. Cut the two 4½"-wide dark green border strips to this length and sew them to the sides of your quilt top, referring to the quilt diagram. Press the seam allowances toward the dark green borders.

5. Sew together two 4½"-wide dark green border strips and press the seam allowances open. Repeat to make another border strip like this. Measure your quilt top horizontally through the center to determine the correct length for the top and bottom inner borders. Cut two 4½"-wide dark green border strips to this length and sew them to the top and bottom edges of your quilt top, referring to the quilt diagram. Press the seam allowances toward the dark green borders.

QUILTING AND FINISHING

1. Press your finished quilt top and mark quilting designs, as desired, referring to Marking Methods on page 30.

2. Prepare the quilt sandwich for quilting, referring to Preparing the Backing on page 29, Layering and Basting on page 31.

3. Quilt by hand or machine, as desired, referring to Hand Quilting on page 31, or Machine Quilting on page 33. The openness of the hourglass blocks makes them a great place to feature many different types of quilting designs. You can quilt inside the triangles to separate the sections visually or choose a floral motif to cover the entire block, as I did. You can also quilt lines that extend from the Hourglass blocks into the Farmer's Daughter blocks.

4. Bind the edges of the quilt and add a hanging sleeve, if desired, referring to Binding on page 33 and Attaching a Hanging Sleeve on page 35.

QUILT SIZES

Lap	64" x 64"
Twin	64" x 84"
King	104" x 104"

BLOCKS IN QUILT

FARMER'S DAUGHTER BLOCKS
Lap	4 light, 1 medium
Twin	6 light, 2 medium
King	16 light, 9 medium

BORDER BLOCKS
Lap	8 light, 4 medium
Twin	10 light, 6 medium
King	16 light, 12 medium

HOURGLASS BLOCKS
Lap	4
Twin	7
King	24

CORNER BLOCKS
Lap	4
Twin	4
King	4

FABRICS AND SUPPLIES

	DARK	CONTRAST	MEDIUM RED	MEDIUM GREEN
Lap	⅜ yard	¼ yard	½ yard	⅔ yard
Twin	⅞ yard	¼ yard	½ yard	⅔ yard
King	1⅜ yards	¾ yard	¾ yard	1⅛ yards

	DARK RED BACKGROUND	DARK GREEN BACKGROUND	LIGHT	MEDIUM TAN
Lap	¾ yard	1⅝ yards	1½ yards	1⅜ yards
Twin	1 yard	2 yards	2 yards	2⅛ yards
King	1¼ yards	2⅝ yards	3¾ yards	3½ yards

CUTTING LIST

	DARKS 2½" x 42" STRIPS	2½" x 2½" SQUARES	CONTRAST 2½" x 42" STRIPS
Lap	3	40	3
Twin	3	64	3
King	10	200	8

	MEDIUM RED TEMPLATE A	TEMPLATE A REVERSED	TEMPLATE B
Lap	12	12	4
Twin	16	16	4
King	28	28	4

	MEDIUM GREEN 6¼" x 6¼" SQUARES	2¼" x 2¼" SQUARES	4" x 4" SQUARES
Lap	8	24	4
Twin	10	32	4
King	16	56	4

	DARK RED 3½" x 42" STRIPS	DARK GREEN 4½" STRIPS	2⅝" BINDING STRIPS
Lap	6	8	7
Twin	8	8	8
King	12	12	10

	LIGHT 2½" x 2½" SQUARES	2½" x 6½" STRIPS	11¼" x 11¼" SQUARES
Lap	16	16	4
Twin	24	24	7
King	64	64	16

	TEMPLATE A	TEMPLATE A REVERSED
Lap	16	16
Twin	20	20
King	32	32

	MEDIUM TAN 2½" x 2½" SQUARES	2½" x 6½" STRIPS	11¼" x 11¼" SQUARES
Lap	4	4	6
twin	8	8	10
King	36	36	22

	5⅞" x 5⅞" SQUARES	6¼" x 6¼" SQUARES
Lap	2	2
Twin	2	2
King	2	2

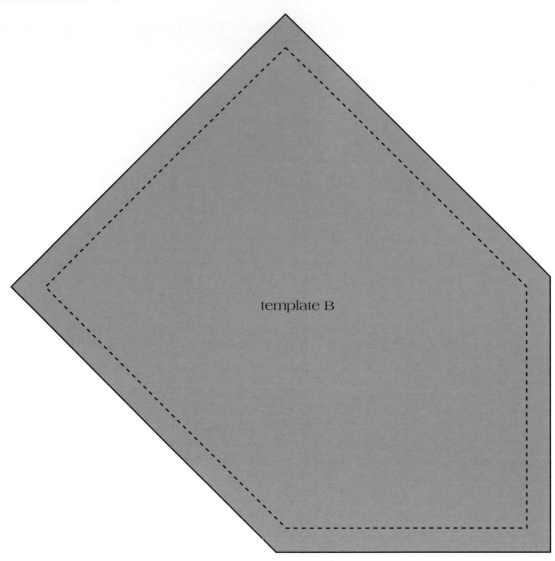

template B

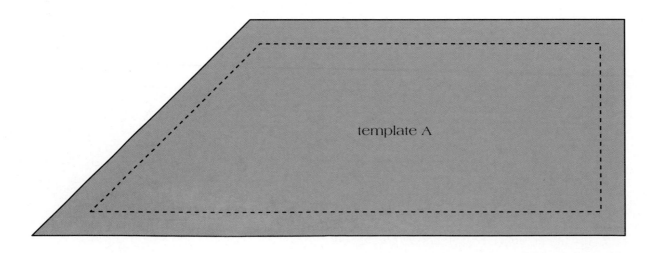

template A

WHIRLWIND

I played with the Curved Log Cabin pattern quite a bit to create this unique design. In addition to this configuration of blocks, you can also arrange your blocks in any traditional Log Cabin setting.

FABRICS AND SUPPLIES

Note: The following instructions are for a queen-size quilt only because any other number of blocks would result in an interruption of the design.

4 yards	total assorted light fabrics for Curved Log Cabin blocks and pieced border
4 yards	total assorted dark fabrics for Curved Log Cabin blocks and pieced border
1½ yards	bright blue fabric for inner border and binding
6½ yards	of fabric for backing
90" x 106"	piece of batting

FINISHED QUILT	84" x 102"
FINISHED BLOCK SIZE	7½" square

CUTTING LIST

FROM THE ASSORTED LIGHT FABRICS:

Cut 50 squares	each 2⅜" x 2⅜".
Cut 80 strips	each 2" x 42".
Cut 36 strips	each 1" x 42".

FROM THE ASSORTED DARK FABRICS:

Cut 34 squares	each 2⅜" x 2⅜".
Cut 36 strips	each 2" x 42".
Cut 36 strips	each 1" x 42".

FROM THE LIGHT AND DARK FABRICS:

Cut 194 strips	each 2" x 8" for pieced border.

FROM THE BRIGHT BLUE FABRIC:

Cut 8 strips	each 2½" x 42" for inner border.
Cut 10 binding strips	each 2⅝" x 42".

To create an even scrappier look for this quilt, use different colors of strips instead of just one color for Step 1.

make 68

make 16

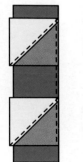

PIECING THE CURVED LOG CABIN BLOCK CENTERS

1. Draw a diagonal line from corner to corner on 42 of the 2⅜" x 2⅜" light squares.

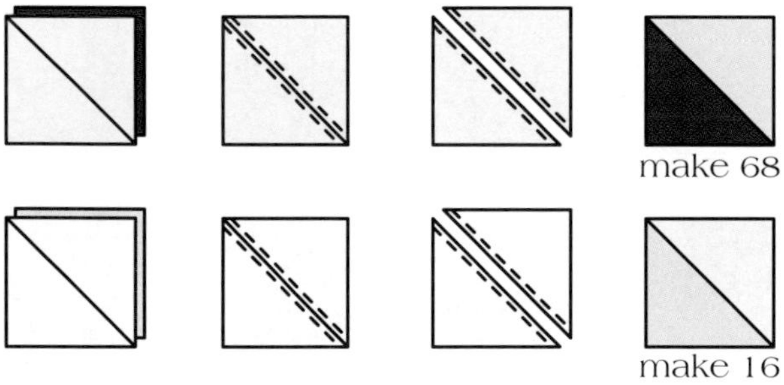

2. Place 34 of the marked 2⅜" x 2⅜" light squares on top of 34 of the 2⅜" x 2⅜" dark squares with right sides together. Place 8 of the marked 2⅜" x 2⅜" light squares on top of the 8 unmarked 2⅜" x 2⅜" light squares with right sides together. Sew a ¼" seam on both sides of the marked lines.

3. Referring to the previous diagram, rotary cut the squares on the marked diagonal lines. Press the seam allowances toward the darker fabrics. Trim the excess fabric at both ends of each seam allowance. You will need a total of 68 light/dark half-square triangle units and 16 light/light half-square triangle units.

PIECING THE MAINLY-DARK CURVED LOG CABIN BLOCKS

1. Place 36 light/dark half-square triangle units on top of 2" x 42" dark strips and sew the squares to the strips. Rotary cut the strips even with the edges of the half-square triangle units, perpendicular to the seam lines. It is important to make these cuts accurately so that your finished blocks will lie flat and true. Press the seam allowances toward the strip fabrics.

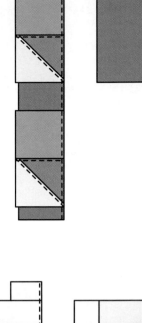

2. Place the Step 1 units right sides together with 2" x 42" dark strips as shown. Sew the Step 1 units to the dark strips. Cut the strips even with the edges of the Step 1 units, perpendicular to the seam lines, making sure that these cuts are accurate. Press the seam allowances away from the Step 1 units.

3. Sew the Step 2 units to 1" x 42" light strips. Note: The seam allowances of the Step 2 units should face your machine. Cut the strips even with the edges of the Step 2 units and press the seam allowances away from the Step 2 units.

4. Sew the Step 3 unit to 1" x 42" light strips. Note: The seam allowances of the Step 3 units should face your machine. Cut the strips even with the edges of the Step 2 units, and press the seam allowances away from the Step 3 units.

5. For the next round, add strips in the order shown. Note: You should always be sewing over two seams. Rotary cut the strip fabrics evenly with the edges of the sewn units as before and press the seam allowances away from the sewn units.

6. For the final round, add strips in the order shown. Rotary cut the strip fabrics evenly with the edges of the sewn units as before and press the seam allowances away from the sewn units. Make a total of 36 mainly-dark Curved Log Cabin blocks.

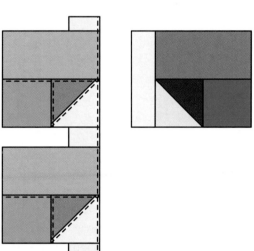

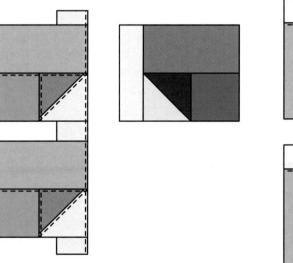

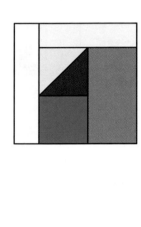

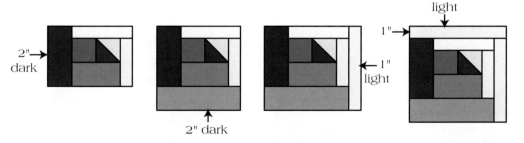

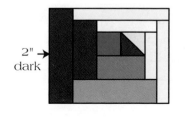

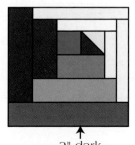

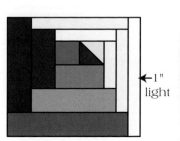

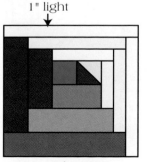

make 36

As for the mainly-dark Curved Log Cabin blocks, you can also increase the scrappy look of your quilt by using different strips for Step 1 rather than using the same color.

PIECING THE MAINLY-LIGHT CURVED LOG CABIN BLOCKS

1. Referring to Piecing the Curved Log Cabin Block Centers on page 74, sew 32 light/dark half-square triangle units to 2" x 42" light strips. Rotary cut the strips even with the edges of the half-square triangle units, perpendicular to the seam lines, and press the seam allowances away from the sewn units.

2. Sew the Step 1 units to 2" x 42" light strips. Note: The seam allowances in the Step 1 units should face your machine. Rotary cut the strips even with the edges of the Step 1 units perpendicular to seam lines and press the seam allowances away from the sewn units as before.

3. Sew the Step 2 units to 1" x 42" dark strips. Note: The seam allowances in the Step 2 units should face your machine. Rotary cut the strips even with the edges of the Step 2 units perpendicular to seam lines and press the seam allowances away from the sewn units as before.

4. Sew the Step 3 units to 1" x 42" dark strips. Note: The seam allowances in the Step 3 units should face your machine. Rotary cut the strips even with the edges of the Step 3 units perpendicular to seam lines and press the seam allowances away from the sewn units as before.

5. For the next round, add strips in the order shown. Note: You should always be sewing over two seams. Rotary cut the strip fabrics even with the edges of the half-square triangle units perpendicular to the seam lines and press the seam allowances away from the sewn units.

6. For the final round, add strips in the order shown. Rotary cut the strip fabrics even with the edges of the half-square triangle units, perpendicular to the seam lines, and press the seam allowances away from the sewn units. Make a total of 32 mainly-light Curved Log Cabin blocks.

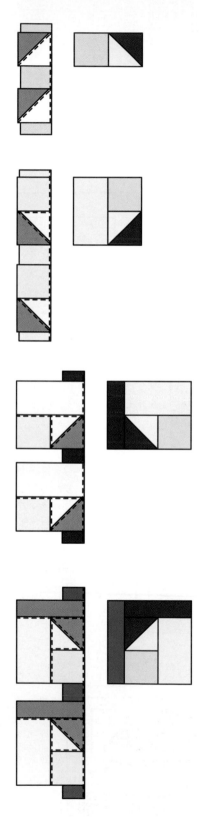

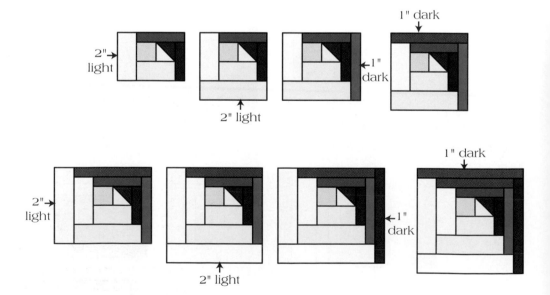

PIECING THE ALL-LIGHT CURVED LOG CABIN BLOCKS

Referring to Piecing the Curved Log Cabin Block Centers and Piecing the Mainly-Dark Curved Log Cabin Blocks on page 74, and Piecing the Mainly-Light Curved Log Cabin Blocks on page 76, sew 16 all-light Curved Log Cabin blocks in the same manner. Start with the 16 light/light half-square triangle units and add 2"-wide and 1" light strips in the order shown.

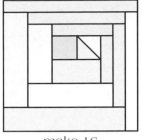

make 16

ASSEMBLING THE QUILT CENTER

Referring to the quilt diagram below, lay out 32 mainly-dark, the 32 mainly-light, and the 16 all-light blocks in quilt in configuration for the quilt center. Sew the blocks together into vertical rows; then sew the vertical rows together.

ADDING THE INNER BORDER

1. Measure your quilt top vertically through the center to determine the correct length for the inner side borders. Note: This length should be 75½"; if your measurement is different, use that number for your side inner border strips and make slight adjustments to your pieced border later. Sew 2 bright blue 2½" x 42" border strips together for each side inner border and cut them to the desired correct measurement.

2. Referring to the quilt diagram, sew the side inner border strips to the quilt center.

3. Measure your quilt top horizontally through the center to determine the correct length for the top and bottom inner borders. Note: This length should be 64½"; if your measurement is different, use your measurement for these border strips and make slight adjustments to your pieced border later. Sew 2 bright blue 2½" x 42" border strips together for each top or bottom inner border and cut them to the desired correct measurement.

4. Referring to the quilt diagram, sew the bright blue top and bottom inner border strips to the quilt center. Press the seam allowances toward the border strips.

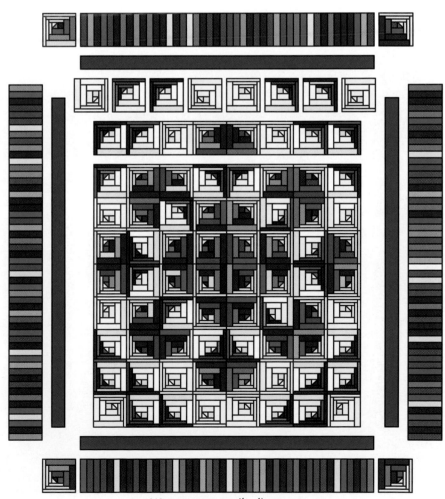

WHIRLWIND quilt diagram

ADDING THE PIECED BORDER

1. Sew the long edges of 53 of the 2"x 8" light and dark strips together for each side border. Pin the side pieced border strips to the quilt center and widen or narrow the seam lines between pieces if necessary to ensure a perfect fit. Referring to the quilt diagram on page 77, sew the pieced side border strips to the sides of the quilt center. Press the seam allowances toward the inner borders.

2. Sew the long edges of 44 of the 2" x 8" light and dark strips together for each of the top and bottom pieced borders. Sew a mainly-dark Curved Log Cabin block to each end of these pieced border strips. Pin the pieced border strips to the top and bottom edges of the quilt center and make any adjustments necessary for fit in the same manner as for the side borders. Referring to the quilt diagram on page 77, sew top and bottom pieced border strips to the quilt center. Press the seam allowances toward the inner borders.

QUILTING AND FINISHING

1. Press your finished quilt top and mark quilting designs, as desired, referring to Marking Methods on page 30.

2. Prepare the quilt sandwich for quilting, referring to Preparing the Backing on page 29, Layering and Basting on page 31.

3. Quilt by hand or machine, as desired, referring to Hand Quilting on page 31, or Machine Quilting on page 33. I quilted an overall design in the light fabrics and did stitch-in-the-ditch outline quilting along the darker strips to accentuate the quilt design.

4. Bind the edges of the quilt and add a hanging sleeve, if desired, referring to Binding on page 33 and Attaching a Hanging Sleeve on page 35.

Curved Log Cabin blocks make a great heart-shaped frame for showcasing some beautiful bleeding heart flowers. I kept my color palette to jewel tones for this quilt and searched for just the right pink to let the blossoms shine out among the other vibrant hues.

FABRICS AND SUPPLIES

1⅛ yards	light blue fabric for block backgrounds and inner border
1 yard	assorted dark blue and purple fabrics for Curved Log Cabin blocks
⅛ yard	bright pink fabric for bleeding heart appliqués
⅛ yard	light pink fabric for bleeding hearts
¼ yard	assorted medium and dark green fabrics for stems and leaves
¼ yard	tan fabric for basket
1 yard	dark blue fabric for outer border and binding
1⅜ yards	of fabric for backing
45" x 40"	piece of batting

FINISHED QUILT	43" x 37½"
FINISHED BLOCK SIZE	5½" square

CUTTING LIST

FROM THE DARK BLUE AND PURPLE FABRICS:

Cut 12 strips	each 1" x 42" strips from 12 different fabrics for Curved Log Cabin blocks.
Cut 2 strips	each 2" x 42" from 12 different fabrics for Curved Log Cabin blocks for a total of 24 strips.
Cut 14 squares	each 2⅜" x 2⅜" for Curved Log Cabin blocks.

FROM THE LIGHT BLUE FABRIC:

Cut 10 strips	each 1" x 42" for Curved Log Cabin blocks.
Cut 6 strips	each 2" x 42" for Curved Log Cabin blocks.
Cut 4 strips	each 2" x 42" for inner border.
Cut 16 squares	each 2⅜" x 2⅜" for Curved Log Cabin blocks.

FROM THE TAN FABRIC:

Cut a 2" x 42" strip for Basket block.
Cut a 2⅜" x 2⅜" square for Basket block.

FROM THE DARK BLUE FABRIC:

Cut 6 strips	each 4" x 42" for outer border.
Cut 4 binding strips	each 2⅝" x 42".

PIECING THE CURVED LOG CABIN BLOCK CENTERS

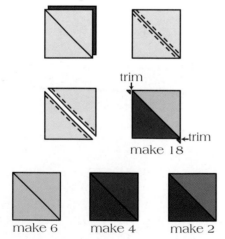

trim

make 18

trim

make 6   make 4   make 2

1. Draw a diagonal line from corner to corner on 13 of the 2⅜" x 2⅜" light squares and 2 of the 2⅜" x 2⅜" dark squares.

2. Place 9 of the marked light blue squares on top of 9 unmarked dark squares, with right sides together. Sew a ¼" seam on both sides of the marked lines. Rotary cut the squares apart on the marked lines between the seams. Trim the excess fabric at each end of the seam allowances and press the seam allowances toward the dark fabrics. You will need a total of 18 of these light-dark half-square triangle units for block centers in the Curved Log Cabin blocks.

3. Place 3 marked light blue squares on top of 3 light blue unmarked squares with right sides together. Referring to Step 2, make a total of 6 light blue-light blue half-square triangle units for block centers.

4. Place the 2 marked dark squares on top of 2 unmarked dark squares with right sides together. Referring to Step 2, make a total of 4 dark-dark half-square triangle units for block centers.

5. Place 1 marked light blue square on top of a tan square with right sides together. Referring to Step 2, make a total of 2 light blue-tan half-square triangle units for block centers.

PIECING THE MAINLY-DARK CURVED LOG CABIN BLOCKS

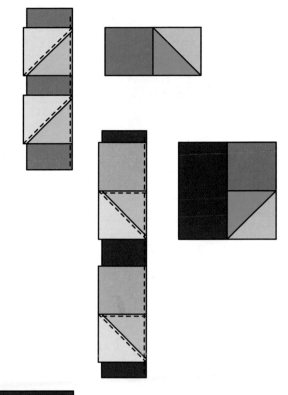

1. Sew 10 light-dark half-square triangle units to a 2" x 42" dark strip. Cut the strip even with the edges of the half-square triangle units and make sure that these cuts are perpendicular to the seams. Press the seam allowances toward the strip fabric. Note: It is important that the perpendicular cut is accurate so that your finished blocks will be flat.

2. Sew the Step 1 units to another 2" x 42" dark strip. Note: The seam allowances in the previously sewn units should face your sewing machine. Cut the strip fabric even with the edges of the units and perpendicular to the seam lines. Press the seam allowances away from the sewn units.

3. Sew the Step 2 units to a 1" x 42" light strip. Note: The seam allowances in the previously sewn units should face your sewing machine. Cut the strip fabric even with the edges of the units and perpendicular to the seam lines. Press the seam allowances away from the sewn units.

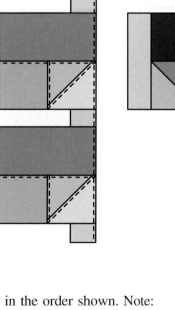

4. Sew the Step 3 units to another 1" x 42" light strip. Note: The seam allowances in the previously sewn units should face your sewing machine. Cut the strip fabric even with the edges of the units and perpendicular to the seam lines. Press the seam allowances away from the sewn units.

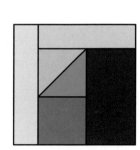

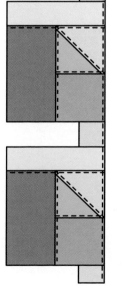

5. Continue adding 1" light and 2" dark strips in the order shown. Note: You should always be sewing over two seams. Cut the units apart accurately, as before and press the seam allowances away from the center of each block. You will need a total of 10 mainly-dark Curved Log Cabin blocks.

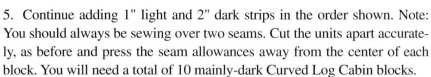

For an even scrappier look, use different dark fabrics rather than the same one throughout.

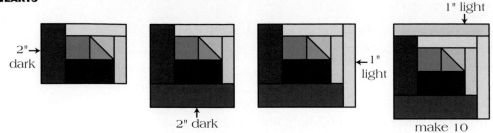

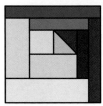

make 8

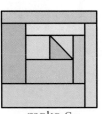

make 6

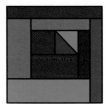

make 4

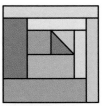

make 2

PIECING THE MAINLY-LIGHT CURVED LOG CABIN BLOCKS

Referring to preceding Steps 1 through 5, make a total of 8 mainly-light Curved Log Cabin blocks, using 1" x 42" dark strips, 2" x 42" light strips, and light-dark half-square triangle units.

PIECING THE LIGHT CURVED LOG CABIN BLOCKS

Referring to preceding Steps 1 through 5, make a total of 6 light Curved Log Cabin blocks, using 1" x 42" light strips, 2" x 42" light strips, and light-light half-square triangle units.

PIECING THE DARK BLOCKS

Referring to preceding Steps 1 through 5, make a total of 4 dark Curved Log Cabin blocks, using 1" x 42" dark strips, 2" x 42" dark strips, and dark-dark half-square triangle units.

PIECING THE BASKET BLOCKS

Referring to preceding Steps 1 through 5, make a total of 2 Basket blocks, using 1" x 42" light blue strips, 2" x 42" tan strips, and tan-light blue half-square triangle units.

ASSEMBLING THE QUILT CENTER

1. Lay out the 10 mainly-dark, 8 mainly-light, 6 light, 4 dark Curved Log Cabin blocks, and the 2 Basket blocks in configuration for the quilt center. Sew the blocks together into vertical rows. Press the seam allowances between blocks in the same direction within each row and in opposite directions in alternating rows.

2. Sew the vertical rows of blocks together, matching intersections, to complete the quilt center. Press the seam allowances between rows in the same direction.

ADDING THE BORDERS

1. Measure your quilt top vertically through the center to determine the correct length for the side inner border strips. Cut 2 light blue 2" x 42" border strips to this measurement and sew them to the sides of the quilt center, referring to Straight Borders on page 26. Press the seam allowances toward the inner borders.

2. Sew together two 2" x 42" light blue strips for each top and bottom inner border. Measure your quilt top horizontally through the center to determine the correct length for the inner border strips. Cut each of the two sewn strips to this length and sew them to the top and bottom edges of the quilt center. Press the seam allowances toward the inner borders.

3. Measure your quilt top vertically through the center to determine the correct length for the side outer border strips. Cut 2 dark blue 4" x 42" border strips to this measurement, and sew them to the sides of the quilt center. Press the seam allowances toward the outer borders.

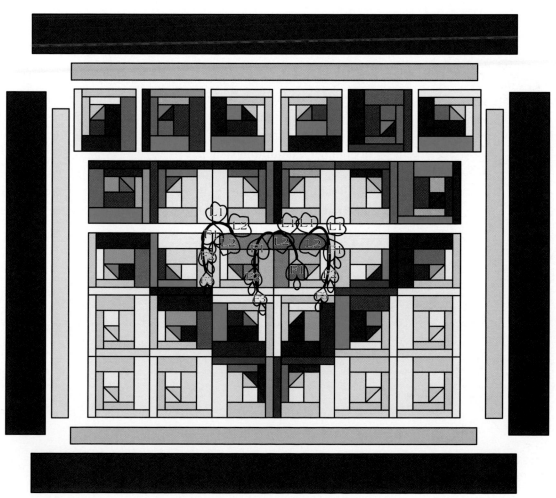

BLEEDING HEARTS quilt diagram

4. Sew together two 4" x 42" dark blue strips for each top and bottom outer border. Measure your quilt top horizontally through the center to determine the correct length for the outer border strips. Cut each of the two sewn strips to this length, and sew them to the top and bottom edges of the quilt center. Press the seam allowances toward the outer borders.

STITCHING THE APPLIQUÉS

1. Referring to Preparing Stems and Vines on page 25 and the quilt diagram for placement, prepare and stitch the stems in place on the quilt center.

2. Referring to The Appliqué Stitch, Outer Points, and Inner Points on pages 23–24, stitch the leaves and flowers in place on the quilt top.

Note: Leaves and flowers should overlap the ends of stems.

QUILTING AND FINISHING

1. Press your finished quilt top and mark quilting designs, as desired, referring to Marking Methods on page 30.

2. Prepare the quilt sandwich for quilting, referring to Preparing the Backing on page 29, Layering and Basting on page 31.

3. Quilt by hand or machine, as desired, referring to Hand Quilting on page 31, or Machine Quilting on page 33. I quilted an overall background pattern on the light blue background areas and outline-quilted the heart and the bleeding heart flowers. The outside border features a quilted motif from a commercial quilting stencil.

4. Bind the edges of the quilt and add a hanging sleeve, if desired, referring to Binding on page 33 and Attaching a Hanging Sleeve on page 35.

flower center

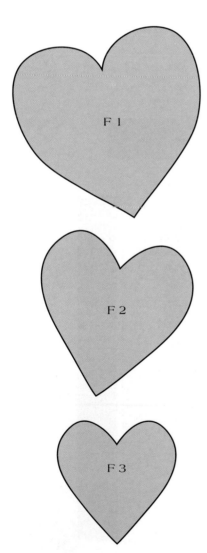

add seam allowances to all pieces as you cut them out

add seam allowances to all
pieces as you cut them out

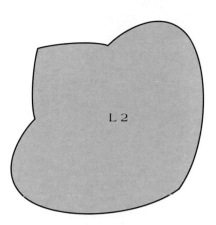

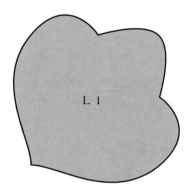

JACK'S CHAIN

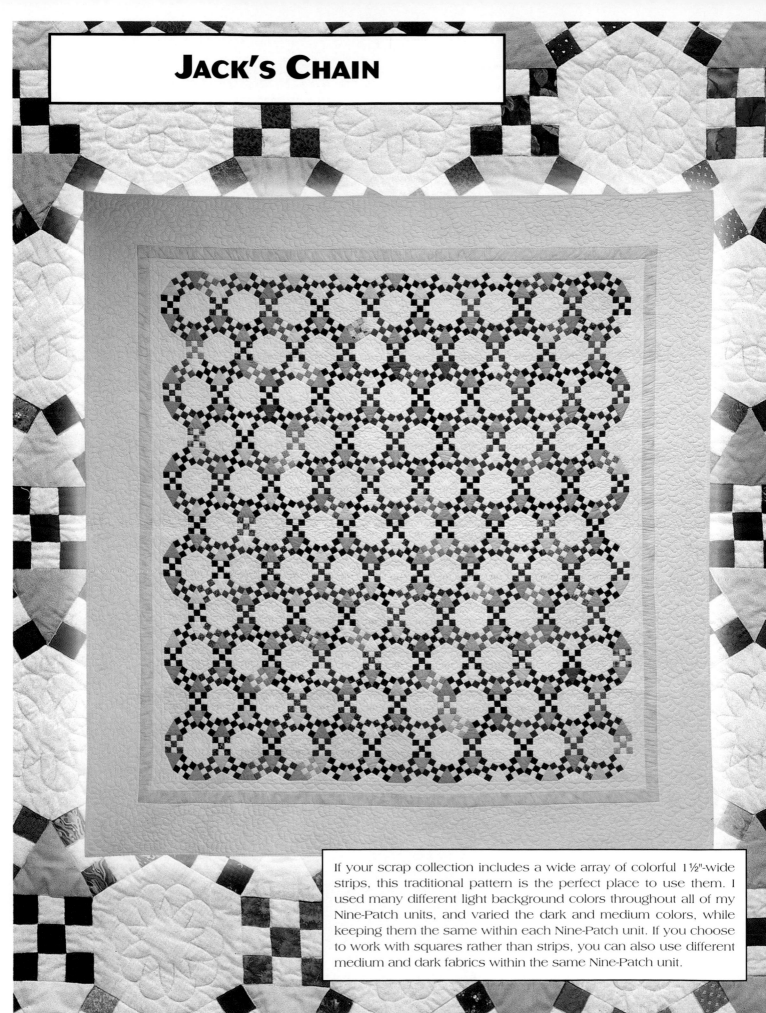

If your scrap collection includes a wide array of colorful 1½"-wide strips, this traditional pattern is the perfect place to use them. I used many different light background colors throughout all of my Nine-Patch units, and varied the dark and medium colors, while keeping them the same within each Nine-Patch unit. If you choose to work with squares rather than strips, you can also use different medium and dark fabrics within the same Nine-Patch unit.

FABRICS AND SUPPLIES

11 yards	light fabric for background, inner border, outer border, and binding
1¾ yards	assorted pastel fabrics for triangles between Nine-Patch units
1⅛ yards	light pink fabric for middle border
3 yards	assorted medium and dark fabrics for Nine-Patch units

FINISHED QUILT	100" x 105"
FINISHED NINE-PATCH UNIT	3" square
FINISHED RING SIZE	approximately 11"

CUTTING LIST

FROM THE LIGHT BACKGROUND FABRIC:

Cut 65 strips	each 1½" x 42" for Nine-Patch units.

Note: Cut each of these strips into two 1½" x 8" strips and one 1½" x 16" strip.

Cut 94 pieces	using Template A.
Cut 10 pieces	using Template C.
Cut 10 pieces	using Template D.
Cut 10 pieces	using Template D reversed.
Cut 4 pieces	using Template E.
Cut 4 pieces	using Template E reversed.
Cut 16 pieces	using Template F.
Cut 12 strips	each 2½" x 42" for inner border.
Cut 12 strips	each 9" x 42" for outer border.
Cut 10 binding strips	each 2⅝" x 42".

FROM THE PASTEL FABRICS:

Cut 228 pieces	using Template B.

FROM THE LIGHT PINK FABRIC:

Cut 12 strips	each 2½" x 42" for middle border.

FROM THE ASSORTED MEDIUM AND DARK FABRICS:

Cut 65 strips	each 1½" x 42" for Nine-Patch units.

Note: Cut each of these strips into two 1½" x 16" strips and one 1½" x 8" strip.

PIECING THE NINE-PATCH UNITS

Note: Use the same-color medium or dark color strips in each Nine-Patch unit. One 1½" x 42" medium or dark strip and one 1½" x 42" light background strip will be enough to make 5 Nine-Patch units.

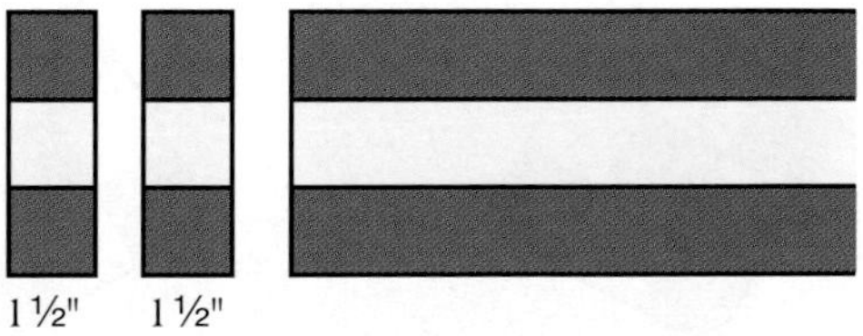

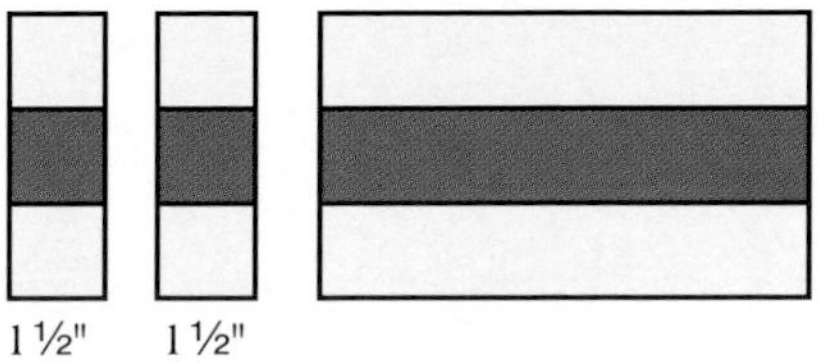

1. Sew the 1½" x 16" medium or dark strips to each side of the 1½" x 16" light background strips. Sew the 1½" x 8" light background strip to each side of a 1½" x 8" medium or dark strip. Press all seam allowances toward the medium or dark fabrics.

2. Rotary cut the strip sets into 1½"-wide segments.

3. Sew together three segments to complete each Nine-Patch unit. Press these seam allowances in opposite directions. Make a total of 321 Nine-Patch units.

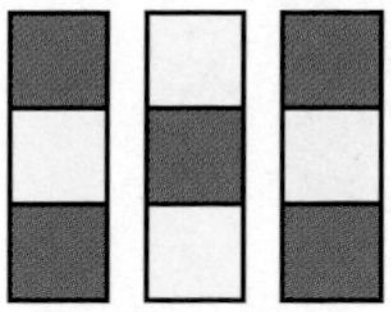
make 321

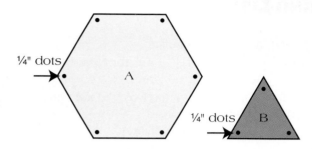

¼" dots

¼" dots

PIECING THE JACK'S CHAIN BLOCKS

1. Mark a dot to indicate the corner points of the ¼" seam lines on all sides of the light background A pieces and the Nine-Patch units. Do the same for the pastel B triangles.

2. Place a pin through the ¼" dots at the corners of the Nine-Patch units and match them to the ¼" dots on the light background A pieces. Referring to "Inset Seams" on page 21, sew one Nine-Patch unit to each of 30 A pieces, beginning and ending each seam exactly at the ¼" dots and backstitching at both ends of the seams to secure the stitching lines.

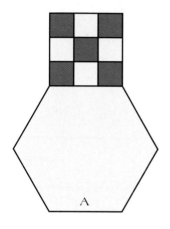

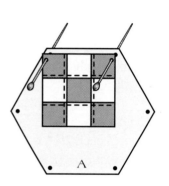 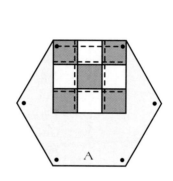

3. Sew two more Nine-Patch units to the 30 A pieces, leaving one edge free between the Nine-Patch units.

4. In the same manner, sew a pastel B triangle to a Nine-Patch unit, referring to "Inset Seams" on page 21. Press the seam allowance toward the B triangle.

5. Sew a pastel B triangle to the opposite side of the Nine-Patch unit. Press the seam allowance toward the B triangle. Make a total of 90 of these units.

6. Match the ¼" points on a Nine-Patch unit from Step 5 to the ¼" marks on one of the unsewn edges of a Jack's Chain block. Referring to "Inset Seams" on page 21, sew between the ¼" marks. Then sew the pastel B triangles to the adjacent Nine-Patch units. Press the seam allowances away from the Nine-Patch units.

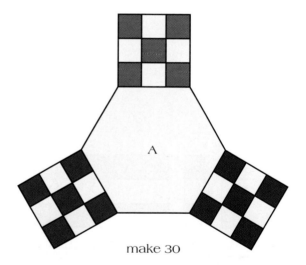

make 30

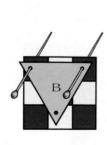  

make 90

7. Continue sewing Step 5 units to the remaining edges of the Jack's Chain block. Make a total of 30 Jack's Chain blocks.

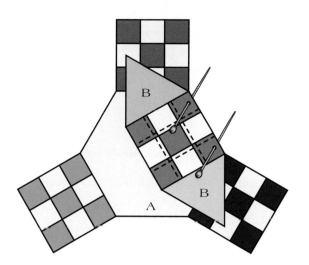

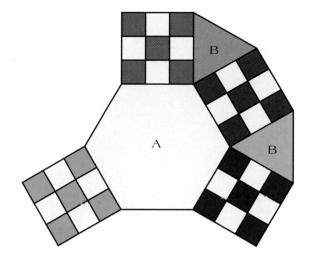

PIECING THE HALF-JACK'S CHAIN BLOCKS

Sew a Nine-Patch unit to either side of a pastel B triangle, starting and stopping at the ¼" marks as before, and press the seam allowances away from the Nine-Patch units. Sew two of these units to opposite sides of a light background A piece. Make a total of 24 Half-Jack's Chain blocks.

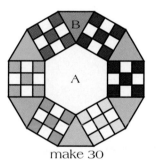

make 30

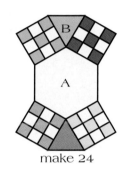

make 24

ASSEMBLING THE QUILT CENTER

1. Lay out the 30 Jack's Chain blocks and 24 Half-Jack's Chain blocks in horizontal rows.

2. Between the rows of Jack's Chain and Half-Jack's Chain blocks, add connecting rows consisting of alternating Nine-Patch units and light background A pieces, referring to the previous diagram.

3. Referring to the previous diagram and to "Inset Seams" on page 21, sew the Jack's Chain and Half-Jack's Chain blocks into horizontal rows. In the same manner, sew the connecting rows together. Finally sew the rows together.

4. For the side filler units, sew a light background D and a Dr piece to a light background C piece as shown on page 90. Press the seam allowances toward the C piece, referring to the same diagram. Make 10 of these side filler units and sew them to the sides of the quilt center, referring to "Inset Seams" on page 21.

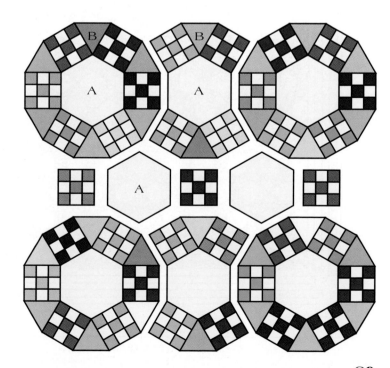

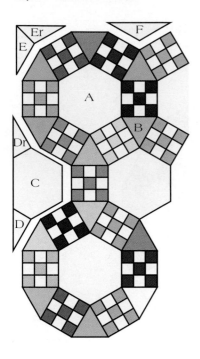

5. At the top and bottom edges of the quilt center, sew light background F pieces between the Nine-Patch units, referring to the previous diagram and to "Inset Seams" on page 21.

6. At each corner, sew a light background E piece to a light background E reversed piece, referring to the previous diagram and to "Inset Seams" on page 21. Sew these units to corners of the quilt center, referring to the previous diagram.

ADDING THE BORDERS

1. Sew three 2½" x 42" light background strips together. Repeat to make a total of 4 of these inner border strips.

2. Measure your quilt top vertically through the center to determine the correct length for the side inner borders. Trim two of the sewn border strips to this measurement and sew them to the sides of the quilt center. Press the seam allowances toward the inner borders.

3. Measure your quilt top horizontally through the center to determine the correct length for the top and bottom inner border strips. Trim the two remaining sewn strips to this length and sew them to the top and bottom edges of the quilt center, referring to the previous diagram.

4. Referring to the previous diagram, repeat Steps 1 through 3 to add the 2½"-wide light pink middle border strips.

5. Referring to the previous diagram, repeat Steps 1 through 3 to add the 9"-wide light background outer border strips. Repeat the above process with the measuring for each border length and sew to quilt.

I used a 9" cut width for the outer border in the quilt shown on page 86 so that I could use a quilting design from a commercial quilting stencil. To use a stencil design, simply adjust the cut width of the outer border strips, making them as wide or as narrow as necessary to accommodate the design's width.

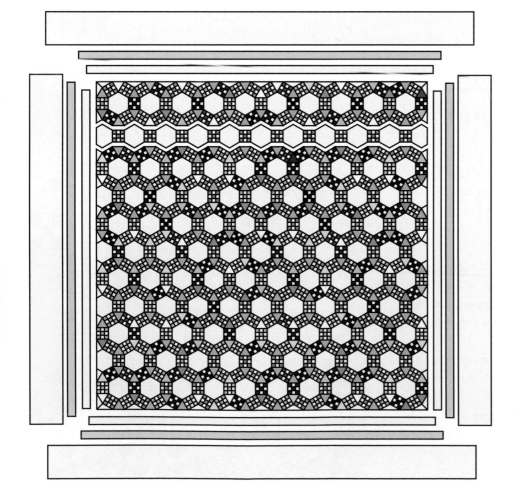

JACK'S CHAIN quilt diagram

QUILTING AND FINISHING

1. Press your finished quilt top and mark quilting designs, as desired, referring to "Marking Methods" on page 30.

2. Prepare the quilt sandwich for quilting, referring to "Preparing the Backing" on page 29, "Layering and Basting" on page 31.

3. Quilt by hand or machine, as desired, referring to "Hand Quilting" on page 31, or "Machine Quilting" on page 33. I quilted in the ditch of the Nine-Patch units as well as the other seams in the design. I chose a stenciled design that would fit in the A pieces and more stenciled designs for the outer border.

4. Bind the edges of the quilt and add a hanging sleeve, if desired, referring to "Binding" on page 33 and "Attaching a Hanging Sleeve" on page 35.

The baby-size Jack's Chain quilt features a partial unit at the end of three rows. To make this end unit, sew a pastel B triangle to each side of a Nine-Patch unit and sew this unit to one side of a light background A piece. Make 3 of these units and add them to the Half-Jack's Chain block at the right end of the top, middle, and bottom rows of the quilt center.

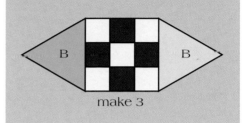

make 3

CUTTING LIST

	LIGHT BACKGROUND			
	TEMPLATE A	*TEMPLATE C*	*TEMPLATE D*	*TEMPLATE D* REVERSED
Baby	18	4	4	4
Twin	41	8	8	8
Full/Queen	72	10	10	10
	TEMPLATE E	*TEMPLATE E* REVERSED	*INNER BORDER* 2½" X 42" STRIPS	*OUTER BORDER* 9" X 42" STRIPS (3½" X 42" FOR BABY QUILT ONLY)
Baby	4	4	4	4
Twin	4	4	8	8
Full/Queen	4	4	8	10
	TEMPLATE F	1½" X 42" STRIPS	*BINDING* 2⅝" X 42"	
Baby	6	15	5	
Twin	8	30	8	
Full/Queen	12	51	10	
	PASTEL *TEMPLATE B*	*MEDIUM/DARK* 1½" X 42" STRIPS	*MIDDLE BORDER* 2½" X 42" STRIPS	
Baby	54	15	4	
Twin	110	30	8	
Full/Queen	180	51	10	

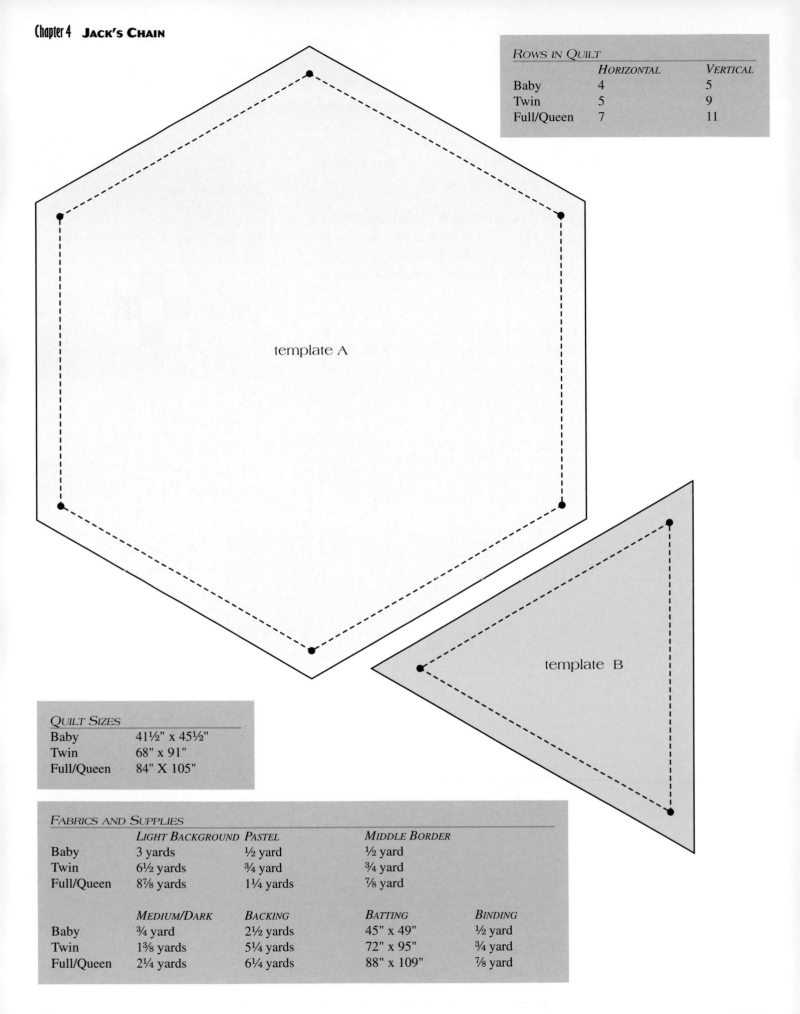

ROWS IN QUILT

	HORIZONTAL	VERTICAL
Baby	4	5
Twin	5	9
Full/Queen	7	11

template A

template B

QUILT SIZES

Baby	41½" x 45½"
Twin	68" x 91"
Full/Queen	84" X 105"

FABRICS AND SUPPLIES

	LIGHT BACKGROUND	PASTEL	MIDDLE BORDER
Baby	3 yards	½ yard	½ yard
Twin	6½ yards	¾ yard	¾ yard
Full/Queen	8⅞ yards	1¼ yards	⅞ yard

	MEDIUM/DARK	BACKING	BATTING	BINDING
Baby	¾ yard	2½ yards	45" x 49"	½ yard
Twin	1⅜ yards	5¼ yards	72" x 95"	¾ yard
Full/Queen	2¼ yards	6¼ yards	88" x 109"	⅞ yard

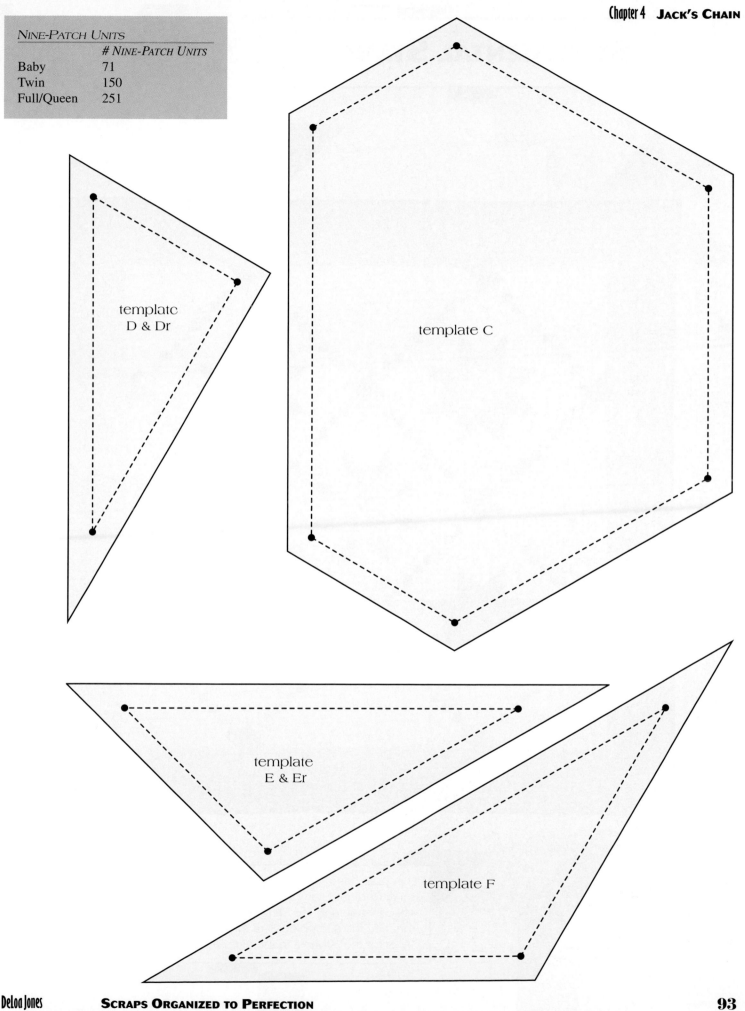

NINE-PATCH UNITS

	# NINE-PATCH UNITS
Baby	71
Twin	150
Full/Queen	251

template
D & Dr

template C

template
E & Er

template F

SENTIMENTAL STARS

This quilt has a planned color scheme with a very scrappy look. Each Radiant Star block features a different color combination while the stars in the Stepping Stones blocks are all red prints. To enhance the scrappiness of this design, I used a range of different darks for the "stones" in the alternate Stepping Stones blocks.

FABRICS AND SUPPLIES

Note: If you are using scrap strips for stars, you will need 1 strip of fabric #1, 2 strips of fabric #2, and 1 strip of fabric #3 for each Radiant Star block.

2⅜ yards	light background fabric for Radiant Star and Stepping Stones blocks
⅜ yard	assorted medium and dark fabrics for Stepping Stones blocks
⅜ yard	of fabric #1 for Radiant Star blocks
¾ yard	of fabric #2 for Radiant Star blocks
⅜ yard	of fabric #3 for Radiant Star blocks
¼ yard	assorted red fabrics for stars in Stepping Stones blocks
1 yard	assorted dark blue fabrics for stars in Stepping Stones blocks and binding
⅞ yard	medium purple fabric for inner border
1¼ yards	medium blue fabric for outer border
4 yards	of fabric for backing
66" x 66"	piece of batting

FINISHED QUILT	61½" x 61½"
FINISHED BLOCK SIZE	11½" square

CUTTING LIST

FROM THE LIGHT BACKGROUND FABRIC:

Cut 5 strips	each 1½" x 42" for Stepping Stones blocks.
Cut 64 squares	each 2½" x 2½" for Stepping Stones blocks.
Cut 64 rectangles	each 1½" x 4½" for Stepping Stones blocks.
Cut 40 rectangles	each 2" x 5½" for Stepping Stones blocks.
Cut 4 rectangles	each 7" x 12" for side rectangles.
Cut 4 squares	7" x 7" for corners.
Cut 20 squares	each 4" x 4" for Radiant Star blocks.
Cut 5 squares	each 6" x 6". Cut these squares diagonally from corner to corner in both directions, for a total of 20 side triangles for Radiant Star blocks.

FROM RADIANT STAR FABRIC #1:

Cut 5 strips	each 1¾" x 42".

FROM RADIANT STAR FABRIC #2:

Cut 10 strips	each 1¾" x 42".

FROM RADIANT STAR FABRIC #3:

Cut 5 strips	each 1¾" x 42".

FROM THE ASSORTED MEDIUM AND DARK FABRICS:

Cut 5 strips	each 1½" x 42" for Stepping Stones blocks.
Cut 32 squares	each 1½" x 1½" for Stepping Stones blocks.

FROM THE ASSORTED RED FABRICS:

Cut 20 squares	each 2" x 2" for stars in Stepping Stones blocks.

FROM THE ASSORTED DARK BLUE FABRICS:

Cut 40 squares	each 2" x 2" for stars in Stepping Stones blocks.
Cut 7 binding strips each 2⅝" x 42".	

FROM THE MEDIUM PURPLE FABRIC:

Cut 8 strips	each 2" x 3½" for inner border.
Cut 4 strips	each 3½" x 12" for inner border.
Cut 4 strips	each 3½" x 15" for inner border.
Cut 4 strips	each 3½" x 22" for inner border.

FROM THE MEDIUM BLUE FABRIC:

Cut 8 strips	each 4½" x 42" for outer border.

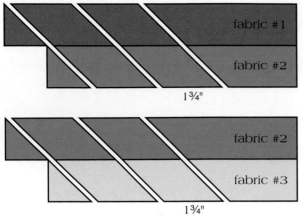

fabric #1

fabric #2

1¾"

fabric #2

fabric #3

1¾"

PIECING THE RADIANT STAR BLOCKS

1. Sew a fabric #1 strip to a fabric #2 strip, offsetting them by 2", as shown. In the same manner, sew a fabric #2 strip to a fabric #3 strip, offsetting them by 2". Press the seam allowances toward fabric #2 in both strip sets.

2. Rotary cut the end of each strip set at a 45-degree angle. Measuring from this end of the strip, rotary cut each strip set into 8 segments, each 1¾" wide.

3. Sew a segment from each strip set together to make a diamond-point, taking care to match the seam intersections. Note: When you pin these two segments together, a small triangle of fabric from the underlying segment will be visible; take care to start and end your stitching line exactly where the two segments intersect, as shown. Press the seam toward the segment that has fabric #3 at the bottom. You will need a total of 8 of these diamond-point units for each Radiant Star block.

4. Mark a ¼" dot at one corner of each diamond-point unit. Referring to Inset Seams on page 21, sew two star point units together, starting at the ¼" dot, and sewing all the way to the other edge of the fabric. Press these seam allowances open. Make 4 of these quarter-star units for each Radiant Star block.

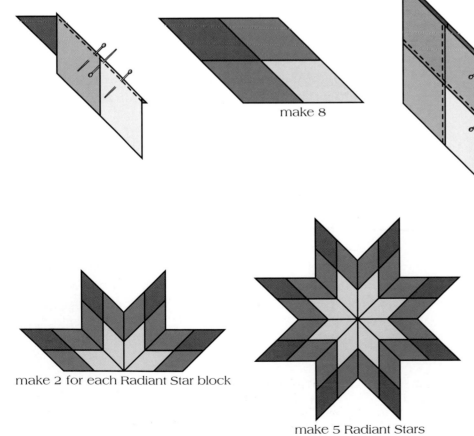

make 8

make 4 for each
Radiant Star block

make 2 for each Radiant Star block

make 5 Radiant Stars

5. Sew 2 quarter-star units from Step 4 together to make a half-star unit, referring to Inset Seams on page 21. You will need to make 2 of these half-star units for each Radiant Star block.

6. Referring to Inset Seams on page 21, sew two half-star units from Step 5 together, starting at one ¼" dot and ending at the other ¼" dot and taking care to match seam intersections.

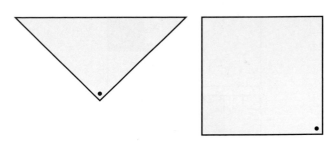

7. Mark a ¼" dot at the right angle of each of the 20 light background side triangles. Also mark a ¼" dot at one corner of the twenty 4" x 4" light background squares.

8. Place a pin at the end of the center seam between two star-point units. Insert the pin through the ¼" dot on a light background side triangle. Sew from the dot to the edge of the star-point unit.

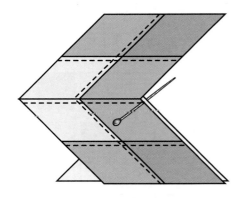

9. Referring to Inset Seams on page 21, sew from the dot to the other edge of the light background triangle. Press the seam allowances toward the star-point units. In the same manner, sew 3 more light background side triangles to the radiant star. Press the seam allowances toward the radiant star.

10. Referring to Inset Seams on page 21, sew the 4" x 4" light background squares to each star, completing the Radiant Star blocks. Make a total of 5 Radiant Star blocks.

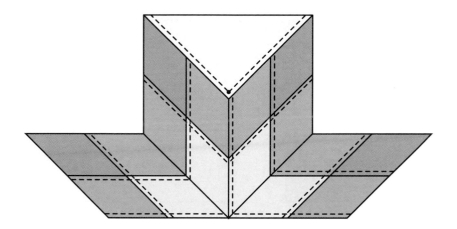

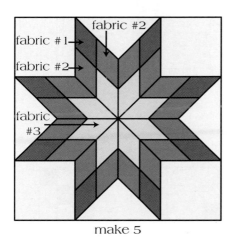

make 5

PIECING THE STEPPING STONES BLOCKS

1. Sew a 1½" x 42" medium or dark strip to a 1½" x 42" light background strip and press the seam allowance toward the darker fabric. Rotary cut this strip set into 1½" segments. Repeat with the remaining light background and medium or dark strips. Cut a total of 128 segments for each Stepping Stones block and Half-Stepping Stones blocks.

1½"

2. Sew 2 segments of different colors together, with the light background fabric in alternating positions. Make a total of 32 of these four-patch units for the Stepping Stones blocks. Make 32 of these four-patch units for the Half-Stepping Stones blocks.

3. Sew 2 four-patch units and two 2½" x 2½" light background squares together. Press the seam allowances toward the light back-

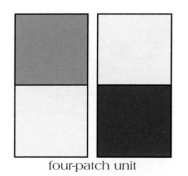

four-patch unit

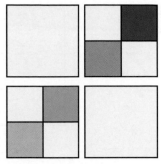

make 4 for each Stepping Stones block
make 2 for each Half-Stepping Stones block

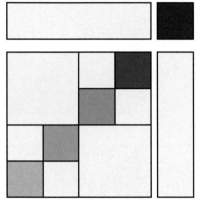

make 4 for each Stepping Stones block
make 2 for each Half-Stepping Stones block

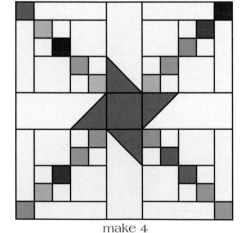

make 4

make 8

ground squares. Make 4 of these units for each Stepping Stones block. Make 2 of these units for each Half-Stepping Stones block.

4. Sew a 1½" x 4½" light background rectangle to a Step 3 unit. Press the seam allowance toward the light background rectangle. Sew a 1½" x 1½" dark or medium square to a 1½" x 4½" light background rectangle and press the seam allowance toward the light rectangle. Sew this unit to a Step 3 unit and press the seam allowance toward the light background rectangle. Make 4 of these units for each Stepping Stones block. Make 2 of these units for each Half-Stepping Stones block.

5. Mark a diagonal line from corner to corner on a 2" red square. Place the marked square on top of a 2" x 5½" light background rectangle with right sides together. Sew exactly on the marked diagonal line. Trim the fabric ¼" from the stitching line and press the seam allowance toward the red fabric. Make 4 of these units for each of the 4 Stepping Stones blocks. Make 3 of these units, using blue 2" squares for each of the 8 Half-Stepping Stones blocks.

make 4 for each Stepping Stones block

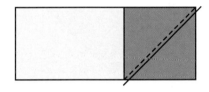

make 3 for each Half-Stepping Stones block

6. Arrange four Step 4 units and four Step 5 units and one 2" x 2" red square in configuration for a Stepping Stones block. Referring to "Chain-Piecing Blocks" on page 22, sew the units together. Make a total of 4 Stepping Stones blocks.

7. For each of the Half-Stepping Stones blocks, sew together 2 Step 4 units, 3 Step 5 units, and a 2" x 2" blue square. Press the seam allowances away from the blue squares. Make 8 of these Half-Stepping Stones blocks.

ASSEMBLING THE QUILT CENTER

Lay out the 5 Radiant Star blocks, 4 Stepping Stones blocks, 8 Half-Stepping Stones blocks, the 7" x 12" light background rectangles, and the 7" x 7" light background squares. Referring to Chain Piecing on page 21, sew the blocks into vertical rows. Then sew the vertical rows of blocks together, completing the quilt center.

ADDING THE INNER PIECED BORDER

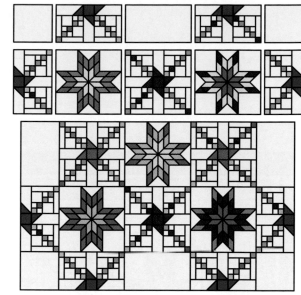

assembling the quilt center

1. Mark a diagonal line from corner to corner on a 2" x 2" dark blue square. Place the marked square on top of a 2" x 3½" medium purple rectangle with right sides together. Sew from corner to corner on the marked diagonal line. Trim the fabric ¼" away from the stitching line and press the seam allowance toward the dark blue triangle. Make 8 of these border star-point units.

2. To sew a side inner border, start by sewing a 3½" x 12" medium purple rectangle to a Step 1 border star-point unit. To the star-point unit, sew a 3½" x 22" medium purple rectangle. To the medium purple rectangle, sew another star-point unit, and finally, add another 3½" x 12" medium purple rectangle. Press the seam allowances toward the medium purple rectangles. Repeat to make a second side inner border, and sew these side inner borders to the sides of the quilt center referring to the quilt diagram on page 100.

3. To sew the top inner border, start by sewing a 3½" x 15" medium purple rectangle to a Step 1 star-point unit. To the star-point unit, sew a 3½" x 22" medium purple rectangle. To the medium purple rectangle, sew another star-point unit, and finally, add another 3½" x 15" medium purple rectangle. Press the seam allowances toward the medium purple rectangles. Make another border just like this one and sew one of the borders to the top edge and one to the bottom edge of the quilt center referring to the quilt diagram on page 100.

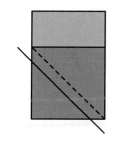
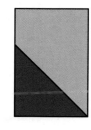

make 2

make 2

ADDING THE OUTER BORDER

1. Sew together two 4½" x 42" medium blue strips for each of the four outer borders.

2. Measure your quilt top vertically through the center to determine the correct length for the side outer border strips. Cut two medium blue border strips to this length and sew them to the sides of the quilt center. Press the seam allowances toward the outer borders.

3. Measure your quilt top horizontally through the center to determine the correct length for the top and bottom outer border strips. Cut the remaining two 4½" x 42" medium blue border strips to this length and sew them to the top and bottom edges of the quilt center, referring to the quilt diagram. Press the seam allowances toward the outer borders.

QUILTING AND FINISHING

1. Press your finished quilt top and mark quilting designs, as desired, referring to Marking Methods on page 30.

2. Prepare the quilt sandwich for quilting, referring to Preparing the Backing on page 29, Layering and Basting on page 31.

3. Quilt by hand or machine, as desired, referring to Hand Quilting on page 31, or Machine Quilting on page 33. I quilted in the ditches of the Radiant Stars and Stepping Stones blocks and used a commercial stencil that I modified for the area around the corner stars. I chose a design from a commercial quilting stencil for the inner pieced border and the outer border.

4. Bind the edges of the quilt and add a hanging sleeve, if desired, referring to Binding on page 33 and Attaching a Hanging Sleeve on page 35.

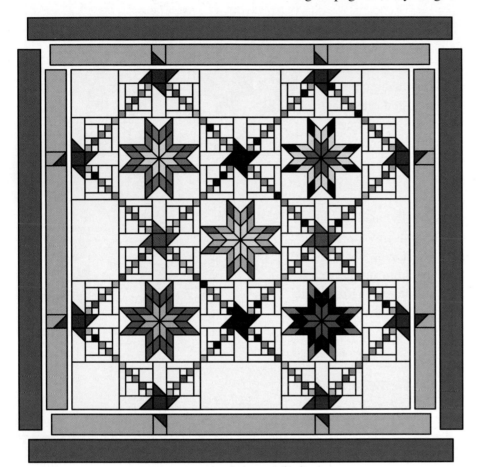

SENTIMENTAL STARS quilt diagram

FABRICS AND SUPPLIES

	LIGHT BACKGROUND	MEDIUMS/ DARKS	RADIANT STAR FABRIC #1	RADIANT STAR FABRIC #2	RADIANT STAR FABRIC #3
Twin	3¼ yards	⅝ yard	½ yard	⅞ yard	½ yard
Full/Queen	5⅞ yards	1 yard	1 yard	1⅞ yards	1 yard
King	7¼ yards	1¼ yards	1⅜ yards	2½ yards	1⅜ yards

	MEDIUM PURPLE	MEDIUM BLUE	ASSORTED REDS	ASSORTED DARK BLUES	BINDING
Twin	1⅛ yards	1¼ yards	¼ yard	¼ yard	¾ yard
Full/Queen	1¾ yards	2 yards	½ yard	½ yard	⅞ yard
King	1⅞ yards	2 yards	¾ yard	¾ yards	1 yard

	BATTING	BACKING
Twin	66" x 85"	6 yards
Full/Queen	89" x 108"	10 yards
King	108" x 108"	10 yards

QUILT SIZES

Twin	61½" x 84½"
Full/Queen	84½" x 107½"
King	107½" x 107½"

RADIANT STAR AND STEPPING STONES BLOCKS

	RADIANT STAR BLOCKS	STEPPING STONES BLOCKS	HALF-STEPPING STONES blocks	BORDER STAR POINTS
Twin	8	7	10	10
Full/Queen	18	17	14	14
King	25	24	16	16

CUTTING LIST

LIGHT BACKGROUND

	1½" x 42" STRIPS	7" x 7" SQUARES	2½" x 2½" SQUARES	1½" x 4½" RECTANGLES
Twin	8	4	96	96
Full/Queen	14	4	192	192
King	19	4	256	256

LIGHT BACKGROUND

	2" x 5½" RECTANGLES	7" x 12" RECTANGLES	4" x 4" SQUARES	6" x 6" SQUARES
Twin	58	6	32	8
Full/Queen	110	10	72	18
King	144	12	100	25

MEDIUM PURPLE

	2" x 3½" RECTANGLES	3½" x 12" RECTANGLES	3½" x 15" RECTANGLES	3½" x 22" RECTANGLES
Twin	10	4	4	6
Full/Queen	14	4	4	10
King	16	4	4	12

	MEDIUM BLUE 4½" x 42" STRIPS	ASSORTED REDS 2" x 2" SQUARES	ASSORTED DARK BLUES 2" x 2" SQUARES
Twin	8	35	50
Full//Queen	12	85	70
King	12	120	80

	FABRIC #1 1¾" x 42" STRIPS	FABRIC #2 1¾" x 42" STRIPS	FABRIC #3 1¾" x 42" STRIPS
Twin	8	16	8
Full/Queen	18	36	18
King	25	50	25

	MEDIUMS/DARKS for STEPPING STONES BLOCKS 1½" x 42" STRIPS	1½" x 1½" SQUARES	BINDING 2⅝" x 42" STRIPS
Twin	8	48	8
Full/Queen	14	96	10
King	19	128	11

ROSE LOG CABIN

The design for this quilt occurred to me as I was piecing WHIRLWIND: CURVED LOG CABIN quilt on page 73. I noticed that the light areas in that quilt looked like roses, so with a quick twist here and there, I had a great starting point for creating this innovative Log Cabin variation.

FABRICS AND SUPPLIES

Note: If you are using pre-cut pieces from your scrap bins, refer to the Cutting List for the number and type of pieces to cut for this project.

⅞ yard	assorted very light fabrics A for Quick-Corner Log Cabin blocks and Rose Log Cabin blocks
⅓ yard	assorted light fabrics B for Quick-Corner Log Cabin blocks
⅓ yard	assorted medium light fabrics C for Quick-Corner Log Cabin blocks
¾ yards	assorted red fabrics for Rose Log Cabin blocks

Note: The red fabrics need to have some differences in value (lightness or darkness) so that the rose "petals" will be visible.

¾ yard	assorted light green fabrics for Quick-Corner Log Cabin blocks
½ yard	assorted dark green fabrics for Quick-Corner Log Cabin blocks and Rose Log Cabin blocks
⅔ yard	medium green fabric for inner border
1½ yards	very dark green fabric for outer border and binding
3 yards	of fabric for backing
54" x 54"	piece of batting

FINISHED QUILT	50" x 50"
FINISHED BLOCK SIZE	9½" square

CUTTING LIST

QUICK CORNER LOG CABIN BLOCKS

FROM THE VERY LIGHT A FABRICS:
Cut eight   1½" x 42" strips.

FROM THE LIGHT B FABRICS:
Cut three   1½" x 42" strips.

FROM THE MEDIUM LIGHT C FABRICS:
Cut two   1½" x 42" strips.

FROM THE LIGHT GREEN FABRICS:
Cut ten   1½" x 42" strips.

FROM THE DARK GREEN FABRICS:
Cut 8 squares   2" x 2".
Cut 72 squares   each 2½"" x 2½".

ROSE LOG CABIN BLOCKS

FROM THE VERY LIGHT A FABRICS:
Cut 24 squares   each 2" x 2".
Cut five   1" x 42" strips.
Cut four   1½" x 42" strips.
Cut 16 squares   each 1½" x 1½".

FROM THE RED FABRICS:
Cut 16 squares   each 2" x 2".
Cut nine   2" x 42" strips.

FROM THE DARK GREEN FABRICS:
Cut 8 rectangles   each 2" x 7½".
Cut 8 rectangles   each 2" x 9".

BORDERS AND BINDING

FROM THE MEDIUM GREEN FABRIC:
Cut eight   2½" x 22" strips for inner border.

FROM THE VERY DARK GREEN FABRIC:
Cut eight   4½" x 42" strips for outer border.
Cut five   2⅝" x 42" binding strips.

PIECING THE QUICK-CORNER LOG CABIN BLOCKS

1. Sew the eight 2" x 2" dark green squares to a 1½" x 42" medium light C strip. Rotary cut the units apart, making sure to cut even with the edges of each square and perpendicular to the seam lines. Press the seam allowances away from the dark green squares.

2. Rotate the Step 1 units, so that the light fabric is on top, and sew them to a 1½" x 42" medium light C strip.

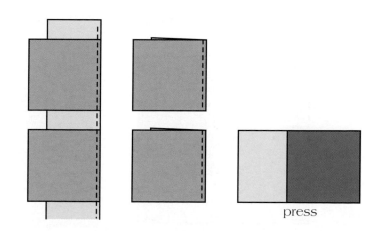

press

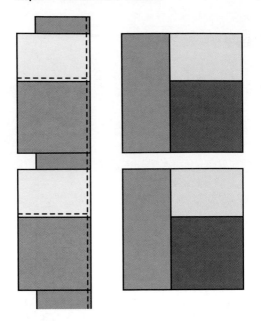

Note: The seam allowances of the Step 1 units should be facing your sewing machine. Rotary cut these units apart as before, and press the seam allowances away from the dark green center squares.

3. Rotate the Step 2 units and sew them to a 1½" x 42" light green strip. Rotary cut these units apart and press the seam allowances away from the dark green center squares, as before.

4. Rotate the Step 3 units and sew them to a 1½" x 42" light green strip. Rotary cut these units apart and press the seam allowances away from the dark green center squares. This completes the first round of each Quick-Corner Log Cabin block.

5. Place a 2½" x 2½" dark green square at the corner of a Step 4 unit, where the medium light C and the light green strips meet. Draw a diagonal line from corner to corner on the dark green square, and sew on the marked line. In the same manner, sew another 2½" x 2½" dark green square at the opposite corner of the Step 4 unit. Repeat for each of the Step 4 units.

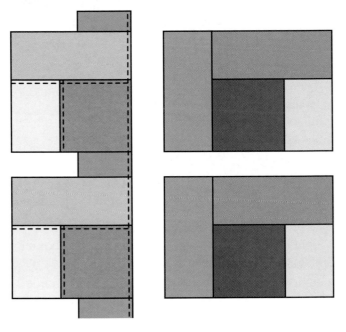

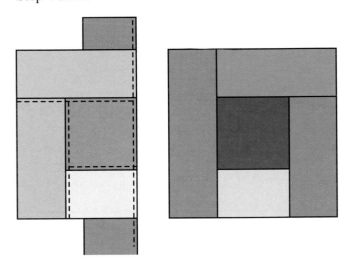

Whenever you sew pieced units to a strip of fabric, it is easier to sew with the strip on the bottom and the units on top, so you can make sure the seam allowances will lie flat as you sew over them.

6. Trim the fabric to ¼" from the sewn lines, and press the triangles open, so that the seam allowances face away from the dark green center squares.

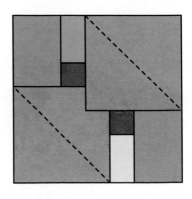
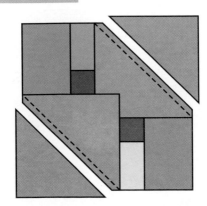
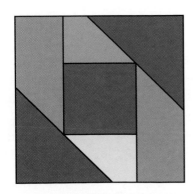

7. For the next round of each block, add 1½"-wide medium light C strips, 1½"-wide light green strips, and 2½" x 2½" dark green squares in the order shown, starting with a 1½" x 42" medium light C strip. Press the seam allowances away from the dark green center squares.

8. For the next round of each block, add 1½"-wide light B strips, 1½"-wide light green strips, and 2½" x 2½" green squares in the order shown, starting with a light B strip. Press the seam allowances away from the dark green center squares.

9. For the next round of each block, add 1½"-wide light A strips, 1½"-wide light green strips, and 2½" x 2½" green squares in the order shown, starting with a light B strip. Press the seam allowances away from the dark green center squares. Make a total of 8 Quick-Corner Log Cabin blocks. The completed blocks should measure 10" square, including the seam allowances.

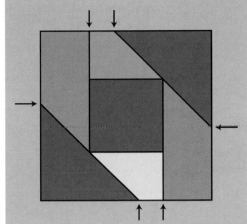

Here is a handy way to always remember where you are as you add the remaining strips to each Quick-Corner Log Cabin block. From this point on, you should always be sewing over at least two seams.

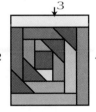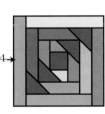

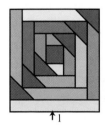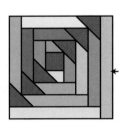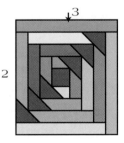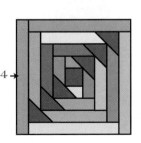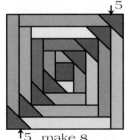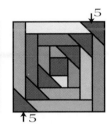

make 8

PIECING THE ROSE LOG CABIN BLOCKS

1. For the centers of the Rose Log Cabin blocks, mark a diagonal line from corner to corner on eight 2" x 2" very light A squares. Place the very light A squares on top of eight 2" x 2" red squares with right sides together, and sew on the marked lines. Trim the fabric to ¼" from the sewn lines, and press the seam allowances toward the red fabric.

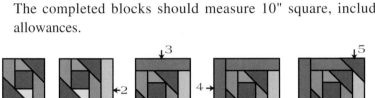

2. Sew the 8 half-square triangle units from Step 1 to eight 2" x 2" red squares. Press the seam allowances away from the center half-square triangle units.

3. Sew the Step 2 units to a 2" x 42" red strip. Rotary cut the units apart, taking care to cut even with the edges of the units and perpendicular to the seam lines. Press the seam allowances away from the center half-square triangle units.

4. Rotate the Step 3 units and sew them to a 1" x 42" very light A strip. Rotary cut these units apart and press the seam allowances away from the center half-square triangle units.

5. Rotate the Step 4 units, and sew them to another 1" x 42" light A strip. Rotary cut these units apart and press the seam allowances away from the center half-square triangle units as before. This completes the first round of the Rose Log Cabin blocks.

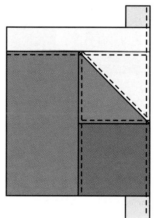

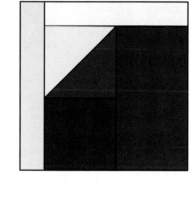

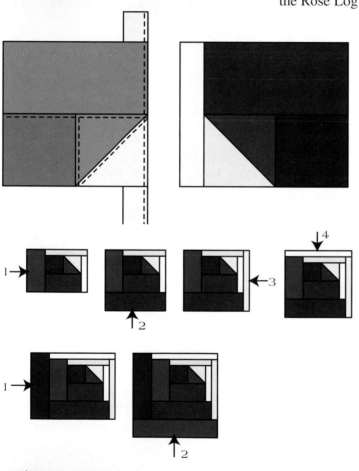

6. For the next round, add 2"-wide red strips and 1"-wide very light A strips in the order shown, starting with a 2"-wide red strip. Press the seam allowances away from the center half-square triangle units.

7. For the next round, add 2"-wide red strips in the order shown. Press the seam allowances away from the center half-square triangle units.

8. Mark a diagonal line from corner to corner on two of the 1½" x 1½" very light A squares. Lay these 1½" x 1½" light A squares at the corners of the 2"-wide red strips you just added. Sew on the marked lines. Trim the fabric to ¼" from the sewn lines, and press the triangles open, so that the seam allowances face the corners of the block. At this point, the block should measure 7½" x 7½"; if it does not, make adjustments to the widths of your seams. Repeat for each Rose Log Cabin block.

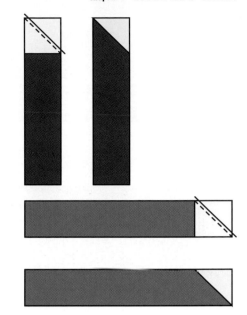

9. Mark a diagonal line from corner to corner on two 2" x 2" very light A squares. Place an A square at one end of a 2" x 7½" dark green strip, and sew on the marked line. Trim the excess fabric to ¼" from the sewn line, and press the seam allowance toward the green strip. Sew a 2" x 2" very light A square at one end of a 2" x 9" dark green strip, so that the seam lies in the opposite direction. Press the seam allowance toward the green strip. Repeat for each Rose Log Cabin block.

10. Sew the shorter units from Step 9 to the left side of each Rose Log Cabin block, and sew the longer units to the adjacent side of each block. Press the seam allowances away from the center half-square triangle unit.

11. Sew a 1½"-wide very light A strip to the two light sides of each Rose Log Cabin block. Make 8 Rose Log Cabin blocks. At this point, the blocks should measure 10" x 10", including the seam allowances. If they do not, adjust the widths of your seam allowances.

 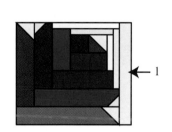 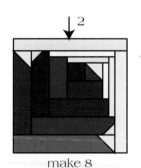

make 8

ASSEMBLING THE QUILT CENTER

Arrange the Rose Log Cabin blocks and the Quick-Corner Log Cabin in vertical rows. Sew the vertical rows of blocks together, and press the seam allowances in each row in alternating directions. Sew the vertical rows of blocks together, completing the quilt center. Press the seam allowances in the same direction.

assembling the quilt center

ADDING THE BORDERS

1. Mark a diagonal line from corner to corner on a 2½" x 2½" dark green square. Place this square at one end of a 2½" x 22" medium green strip with right sides together, and sew on the marked line. Trim the fabric to ¼" from the sewn line, and press the triangle open, so that the seam allowance lies toward the dark green fabric. Make 4 of these units.

2. Sew a 2½" x 2½" dark green square to the other end of the remaining four 2½" x 22" medium green strips, making sure that the seams lie in the opposite direction of the Step 1 units. Make 4 of these units.

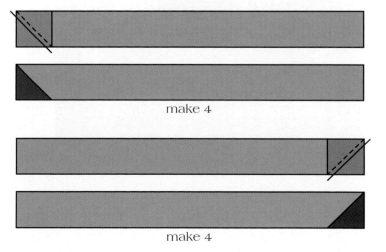

make 4

make 4

3. Sew a Step 1 and a Step 2 unit together, with the dark green triangles together, and press the seam allowance to one side. Make 4 of these pieced inner border strips.

make 4

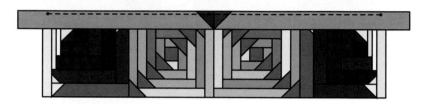

4. Measure 19" in both directions from the center seam of each pieced inner border strip, and mark a dot to indicate the beginning and end of each seam line. Matching the dots on the border strips to the ¼" points on the quilt center, sew the inner border strips to the sides of the quilt center, matching the center triangles. Press the seam allowances toward the inner border strips. Note: Do not cut the excess fabric at the ends of the pieced inner border strips.

5. Sew two 4½" x 42" very dark green strips together for each of the four outer borders. Press these seam allowances open. Matching the center seams of the outer border strips to the center seams of the pieced inner border strips, sew the outer border strips to the pieced inner border strips. Note: Do not cut the excess fabric at the ends of the outer border strips.

6. Referring to Mitered Corners on page 27, sew the four border corner seams. Trim the fabric to ¼" from the sewn seams, and press these seam allowances open.

QUILTING AND FINISHING

1. Press your finished quilt top and mark quilting designs, as desired, referring to Marking Methods on page 30.

2. Prepare the quilt sandwich for quilting, referring to Preparing the Backing on page 29, Layering and Basting on page 31.

3. Quilt by hand or machine, as desired, referring to Hand Quilting on page 31, or Machine Quilting on page 33. I quilted the light areas with an overall background design and stitched in-the-ditch of the triangles and Rose Log Cabin blocks.

4. Bind the edges of the quilt and add a hanging sleeve, if desired, referring to Binding on page 33 and Attaching a Hanging Sleeve on page 35.

ROSE LOG CABIN quilt diagram

AUTUMN IN FULL BLOOM

This design is a wonderful canvas for exploring creative color palettes. Check out the color schemes in the same pattern in SPRING IN FULL BLOOM, page 125, SUMMER BLOSSOMS, page 126, CHRISTMAS IN FULL BLOOM, page 125, and WINTER, page 125.

FABRICS AND SUPPLIES

Note: If you are using pre-cut pieces from your scrap bins, refer to the Cutting List below for the number and type of pieces to cut for this project.

2¾ yards	light background fabric for Center block, Squares and Angles blocks, and Border blocks
1½ yards	assorted red, rust, orange, tan, and gold fabrics for Center block, Squares and Angles blocks, and Border blocks
½ yard	assorted green fabrics for Center block
1⅞ yards	dark green fabric for Border blocks, borders, and binding
3½ yards	of fabric for backing
60" x 60"	piece of batting

FINISHED QUILT	56" x 56"
FINISHED FLOWER BLOCK SIZE	9" square

CUTTING LIST

CENTER BLOCK

FROM THE LIGHT BACKGROUND FABRIC:

Cut 12 squares	each 3⅛" x 3⅛".
Cut three squares	each 5" x 5". Cut these squares diagonally from corner to corner in both directions, for a total of 12 triangles.
Cut one	9½" x 9½" square.

FROM THE RED, RUST, ORANGE, TAN, AND GOLD FABRICS:

Cut 18 pieces	using Template A. For each flower cut three A pieces in one fabric and three A pieces in a contrasting fabric.
Cut 21 squares	each 2½" x 2½", using a different color for each flower (7 squares per flower).

FROM THE GREEN FABRICS:

Cut 2 of Template A	using a different fabric for each flower for a total of 6.
Cut one	1¼" x 15" bias strip for center stem.

Cut two	1¼" x 9" bias strips side stems.
Cut one	4" x 4" square.
Cut 2 pieces	using Template B, for leaves.

CORNER-UNIT BLOCKS

FROM THE LIGHT BACKGROUND FABRIC:

Cut 72 squares	each 2⅜" x 2⅜". Cut these squares diagonally from corner to corner for a total of 144 triangles.

FROM THE RED, RUST, ORANGE, AND GOLD FABRICS:

Cut 36 squares	each 3⅞" x 3⅞". Cut these squares diagonally from corner to corner for a total of 72 triangles.
Cut 72 squares	each 2" x 2".

BORDER BLOCKS

FROM THE LIGHT BACKGROUND FABRIC:

Cut 28 squares	each 3⅛" x 3⅛".
Cut 56 rectangles	each 2" x 5".
Cut 28 squares	each 2" x 2".
Cut 28 squares	each 2¾" x 2¾". Cut each of these squares diagonally from corner to corner.

FROM THE RED, RUST, GOLD, AND ORANGE FABRICS:

Cut 56 pieces	using Template A.
Cut 28 squares	each 2½" x 2½" for for prairie points.

FROM THE DARK GREEN FABRICS:

Cut 56 squares	each 2" x 2".

BORDER STRIPS

FROM THE LIGHT BACKGROUND FABRIC:

Cut two	2½" x 42" strips.
Cut 28 spacer strips	each 1" x 6½".

FROM THE DARK GREEN FABRIC:

Cut four	2¼" x 42" strips.
Cut twelve	2½" x 42" strips.

PIECING THE CENTER BLOCKS

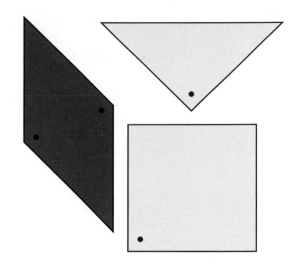

1. Mark a ¼" dot on the 6 green A pieces, the 18 red, rust, gold, and orange A pieces, the 12 light background triangles, and the 12 light background squares, as shown.

2. Select three A pieces in one color, three A pieces in a contrasting color, and 2 green A pieces for each flower unit in the center block. Referring to Inset Seams on page 21, sew two different colored A pieces together, beginning at the ¼" dot and sewing through the seam allowance at the bottom. Make 3 of these units for each flower. In the same manner, sew together two green A pieces for each flower unit. Press the seam allowances in the same direction.

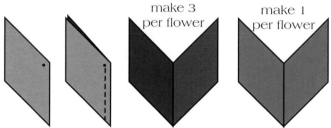

make 3
per flower

make 1
per flower

3. Sew two Step 2 red, rust, gold, or orange units together to create half of each flower unit, beginning at the ¼" dot and sewing through the seam allowance at the bottom edge. Sew together one green unit from Step 2 and the remaining red, rust, gold, or orange Step 2 unit to create the other half of each flower unit. Press the seam allowances in the same direction.

4. Referring to Matching and Pinning Tips on page 17, pin the two halves of each flower unit together, matching the centers. Sew the halves of each flower unit together, starting and ending the seam at the ¼" dots.

5. To make the prairie points for each flower unit, fold the 2½" squares in half diagonally and press the folds. Fold the corners down to the middle, and press the completed prairie points. Make a total of 7 prairie points for each flower unit.

6. For the middle flower unit, place a prairie point at the right angle of 4 light background triangles, and at the corner of 3 light background squares. For each of the two side flower units, place a prairie point on 4 light background

make 7 for each
flower unit

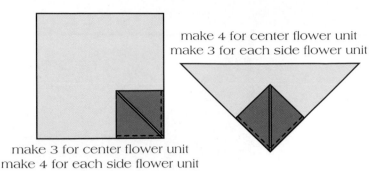

make 4 for center flower unit
make 3 for each side flower unit

make 3 for center flower unit
make 4 for each side flower unit

squares and 3 light background triangles. Staystitch the prairie points in place approximately ⅛" in from the edges of each piece.

7. To prepare the stems, fold the 1¼" x 15" green bias strip and the two 1¼" x 9" bias strips in half lengthwise, with wrong sides together. Sew ¼" in from the raw edges of each stem. Trim the seam allowances to ⅛" and press each stem, centering the seam allowances on the underneath side.

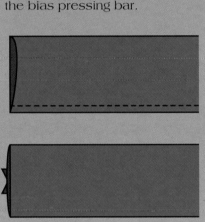

Note: Using a metal or plastic bias bar can make this process easier. Simply slip the bias pressing bar inside the stitched stem with the seam allowance underneath, press, and remove the bias pressing bar.

8. Staystitch one end of the 15" green stem to a light background square for the middle flower unit, taking care to keep this stitching ⅛" in from the edge of the fabric. In the same manner, staystitch the 9" green stems on the remaining two light background triangles for the side flower units. This will allow you to sew the stems into the seams of the center block and appliqué the remaining portion of each stem after the center block is assembled.

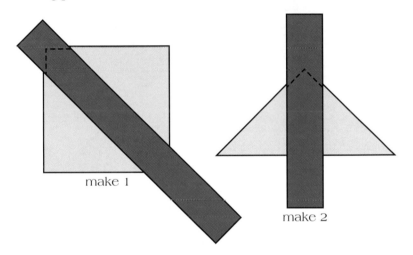

make 1

make 2

9. Referring to Inset Seams on page 21, sew 4 light background triangles with prairie points to the middle flower unit, starting at the ¼" dots and sewing through the outside seam allowance on each side of the triangles. In the same manner, sew 3 light background squares with prairie points to the middle flower unit. To complete the middle flower, sew the light background square with the 15" green stem between the two green A pieces.

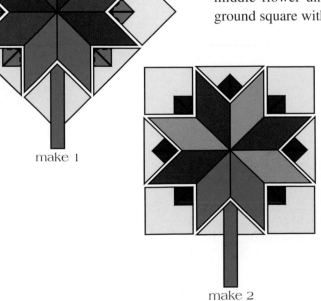

make 1

make 2

10. Referring to Inset Seams on page 21, sew 3 light background triangles with prairie points to each of the two side flower units, starting at the ¼" dots and sewing through the outside seam allowance on each side of the triangles. In the same manner, sew 4 light background squares with prairie points to the flower unit. Sew the light background triangles with the 9" green stems between the two green A pieces of each side flower unit.

ASSEMBLING THE QUILT CENTER

1. Sew the middle and one side flower block together. Sew the remaining side flower block to the flower base unit. Press the seam allowances between the blocks in opposite directions. Sew the final seam, taking care not to catch the unsewn portions of the stems in this seam. Press the seam allowance to one side.

2. Appliqué the two side stems on the light background fabric so they will meet each other underneath the center stem. Appliqué the center stem, covering the ends of the side stems. Mark a diagonal line from corner to corner on the 4" dark green square. Place the dark green square on the bottom light background square, covering the end of the center stem. Sew on the marked diagonal line, trim the fabric to ¼" from the sewn line, and press the seam allowance toward the dark green triangle. Appliqué two green B leaves next to the center stem.

3. Sew a 2½" x 24" light background strip to a 2¼" x 29" green strip, matching the centers. Press the seam allowance open. Make three more of these border strips. Matching the centers, sew this border strip to the Center block, referring to Inset Seams on page 21, and starting and ending ¼" in from the edge of the Center block. Mark a 45° diagonal line at each end of the border strip, starting at the beginning and end of the seam line and going outward to the edge of the border strip. Add a border strip to the remaining three sides of the Center block.

4. Referring to Mitered Corners on page 27, sew the four border corner seams. Trim the excess fabric to ¼" and press these seams open.

5. Sew a light background triangle to a 2" rust, red, gold or orange square. Press the seam allowance toward the light background triangle. Sew another light background triangle to the adjacent side of the same 2" square. Press the seam allowance toward the light background triangle. Make 72 of these units.

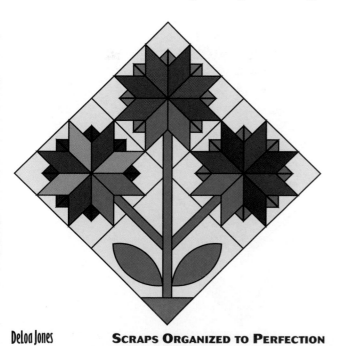

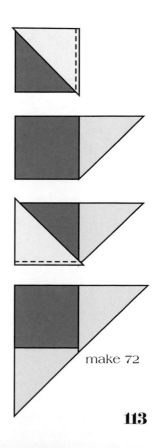

make 72

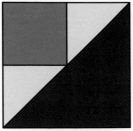

make 60

6. Sew a rust, red, gold or orange triangle to 60 of the Step 1 units. Press the seam allowances toward the triangles.

7. Arrange 15 Step 6 units, 3 Step 5 units, and 3 red, rust, orange, or gold triangles, as shown, for each corner of the quilt center. Referring to Chain-Piecing on page 21, sew the units together into vertical rows. Press the seam allowances between units in the same direction, and in alternating directions in each vertical row. Sew the vertical rows of units together, and press the seam allowances between rows in the same direction. Make three more of these corner units.

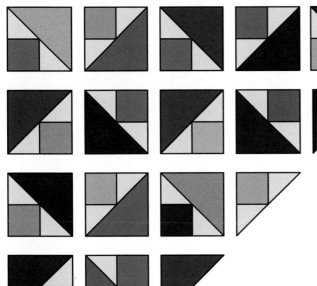

make 4

8. Sew a Step 7 corner unit to each side of the quilt center, and press the seam allowances toward the dark green borders.

9. Measure your quilt top vertically through the center to determine the correct length for the green border strips. Cut two 2½"-wide green border strips to this measurement. Referring to the quilt diagram on page 116, sew them to the sides of the quilt center. Press the seam allowances toward the green border strips.

10. Measure your quilt top horizontally through the center to determine the correct length for the top and bottom border strips. Cut two 2½"-wide green border strips to this measurement, and sew them to the top and bottom edges of the quilt center. Press the seam allowances toward the green border strips.

ADDING THE PIECED BORDER

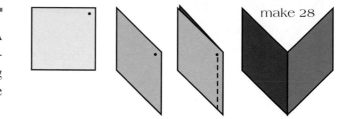

make 28

1. Mark the ¼" point on the 56 red, rust, orange, tan, and gold A pieces and the twenty-eight 3⅛" light background squares. Referring to Inset Seams on page 21, sew two A pieces together, starting the seam at the ¼" point and sewing through the seam allowance at the other end. Make 28 of these units.

2. Sew a light background triangle to each side of the Step 1 units.

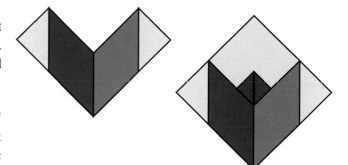

3. Referring to Steps 5 and 6 on page 111, make a prairie point and stay-stitch it to one corner of a 3⅛" light background square. Referring to Inset Seams on page 21, sew this light background square between the A pieces. Make 28 of these units.

make 28

4. Draw a diagonal line from corner to corner on each of the 2" green squares. Lay a 2" green square at one end of a 2" x 5" light background rectangle, and sew on the marked line. Trim the fabric to ¼" from the sewn line, and press the seam allowance toward the green fabric. Make 28 of these units.

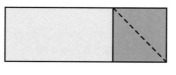  

make 28

5. In the same manner, sew a 2" square to the end of a 2" x 5" light background rectangle, with the seam going in the opposite direction. Trim the fabric to ¼" from the sewn line, and press the seam allowance toward the green fabric. Make 28 of these units.

make 28

6. Sew a Step 3 unit, a Step 4 unit, a Step 5 unit, and a 2" light background square together to complete each Border block. Press the seam allowances toward the outer edges of the block. Make 28 Border blocks.

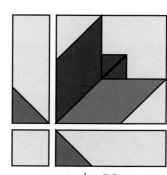

make 28

7. Sew together 6 Border blocks and seven 1" x 6½" light background strips. Press the seam allowances to the 1" strip. Make three more of these pieced border units. Sew two of these pieced border units to the sides of the quilt center, and press the seam allowances toward the dark green borders.

8. Sew a Border block to each end of the remaining two pieced border units. Sew these pieced border units to the top and bottom edges of the quilt center, matching the mid-points. Press the seam allowances toward the dark green borders.

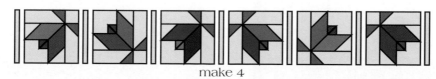

make 4

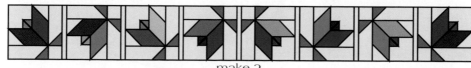

make 2

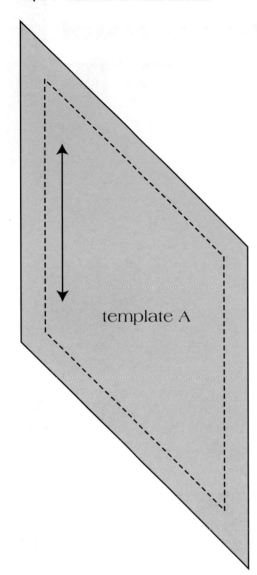

template A

ADDING THE OUTER BORDER

1. Sew together two 2½" x 42" dark green strips. Make three more of these outer border strips.

2. Measure your quilt top vertically through the center to determine the correct length for the side border strips. Cut two of the 2½"-wide dark green border strips to this measurement, and sew them to the sides of the quilt center. Press the seam allowances toward the dark green border strips.

3. Measure your quilt top horizontally through the center to determine the correct length for the top and bottom outer border strips. Cut the remaining two 2½"-wide dark green border strips to this measurement and sew them to the top and bottom edges of the quilt center. Press the seam allowances toward the dark green outer border strips.

QUILTING AND FINISHING

1. Press your finished quilt top and mark quilting designs, as desired, referring to Marking Methods on page 30.

2. Prepare the quilt sandwich for quilting, referring to Preparing the Backing on page 29, Layering and Basting on page 31.

3. Quilt by hand or machine, as desired, referring to Hand Quilting on page 31, or Machine Quilting on page 33. I quilted a meandering background pattern in the light background areas of the quilt center and the border blocks, and stitched in the ditch of the patchwork seams.

4. Bind the edges of the quilt and add a hanging sleeve, if desired, referring to Binding on page 33 and Attaching a Hanging Sleeve on page 35.

AUTUMN IN FULL BLOOM quilt diagram

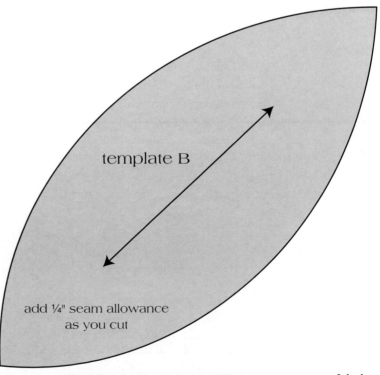

template B

add ¼" seam allowance
as you cut

If you're looking for a project where you can use a lot of 1½"-wide short scrap strips, or 1½" squares from your scrap bins, the Goose-in-the-Pond blocks in this quilt are for you! You can also cut 42"-long strips – either way, the result will be a striking scrap quilt.

FABRICS AND SUPPLIES

Note: If you are making this quilt in the other size, refer to the charts on page 122 for Quilt Size, Fabrics and Supplies, and Cutting List.

6 yards	light background fabric for Goose-in-the-Pond blocks and Rail Fence units, sashings, pieced border, outer border, and binding
2¼ yards	assorted pink fabrics for Goose-in-the-Pond blocks, Rail Fence units, and pieced border
½ yard	assorted pastel fabrics for Nine-Patch units.
½ yard	assorted tan fabrics for Rail Fence units and Goose-in-the-Pond block centers.
6½ yards	of fabric for backing
75" x 93"	piece of batting

FINISHED QUILT	71" x 89"
FINISHED BLOCK SIZE	15" square

CUTTING LIST

FROM THE LIGHT BACKGROUND FABRIC:

Cut thirteen	1½" x 42" strips for Nine-Patch units in Goose-in-the-Pond blocks and sashings.
Cut 72 squares	each 3⅞" x 3⅞" for Goose-in-the-Pond blocks.
Cut 48 squares	each 3½" x 3½" for Goose-in-the-Pond blocks.
Cut 31 strips	each 3½" x 15½" for sashings.
Cut 44 squares	each 3⅞" x 3⅞" for pieced border.
Cut 4 squares	each 3½" x 3½" for pieced border.
Cut 10 strips	each 4½" x 42" for outer border.
Cut 8 binding strips	each 2⅝" x 42".

FROM THE ASSORTED TAN FABRICS:

Cut five	1½" x 42" strips for Rail Fence units.
Cut 12 squares	each 3½" x 3½" for Goose-in-the-Pond blocks.

FROM THE ASSORTED PASTEL FABRICS:

Cut eleven	1½" x 42" strips for Nine-Patch units, Goose-in-the-Pond blocks, and sashings.

FROM THE PINK FABRICS:

Cut ten	1½" x 42" strips for Rail Fence units.
Cut 72 squares	each 3⅞" x 3⅞" for Goose-in-the-Pond blocks.
Cut 44 squares	each 3⅞" x 3⅞" for pieced border.

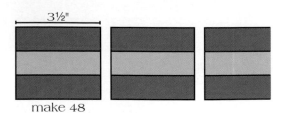

3½"

make 48

PIECING THE RAIL FENCE UNITS

Note: If you wish to make all your Rail Fence units in the same fabrics, two 42"-long strips in one color and one 42"-long strip in a second color will be enough to make 10 Rail Fence units. If you use 1½"-wide scrap strips in varying lengths, each strip will need to be at least 3½" long.

1. Sew two 1½" x 42" pink strips to each side of a 1½"-wide tan strip. Make 5 of these strip sets. Press the seam allowances toward the pink strips.

2. Rotary cut the strip sets into 48 segments, each 3½" wide. Note: If you wish, you can cut the leftover portion of the last strip set into 1½"-wide segments and use them for Nine-Patch units later.

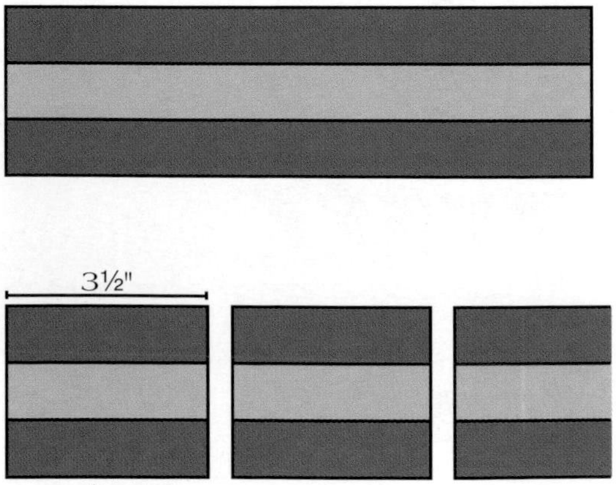

PIECING THE NINE-PATCH UNITS

1. Sew two 1½" x 42" pastel strips to each side of a 1½" x 42" light background strip. Make 3 of these strip sets. Press the seam allowances toward the pastel strips. Rotary cut these strip sets into 68 segments, each 1½" wide.

2. Sew two 1½" x 42" light background strips to each side of a 1½" x 42" pastel strip, referring to Step 1 under Piecing the Rail Fence Units on page 118. Make 5 of these strip sets. Press the seam allowances toward the pastel strips. Rotary cut these strip sets into 136 segments, each 1½" wide.

3. Sew the Step 1 and Step 2 units together for each Nine-Patch unit, matching the seam intersections. Make 68 Nine-Patch units; 48 for the Goose-in-the-Pond blocks and 20 for the sashings. Press the seam allowances open.

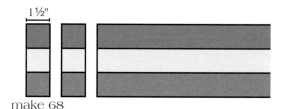

make 68

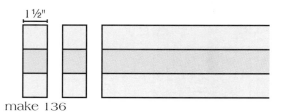

make 136

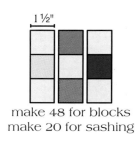

make 48 for blocks
make 20 for sashing

PIECING THE HALF-SQUARE TRIANGLE UNITS

Note: For each Goose-in-the-Pond block, you will need six 3⅞" half-square triangle units. They can be identical, as in my quilt, or scrappy, as desired.

1. Mark a diagonal line from corner to corner on seventy-two 3⅞" light background squares. Place the 3⅞" light background squares right sides together with the 3⅞" pink squares.

2. On each pair of squares, sew ¼" away from the marked line on both sides. Rotary cut on the marked lines, for a total of 144 half-square triangle units. Trim the excess fabric at the ends of the seam allowances, and press the seam allowances toward the pink fabric.

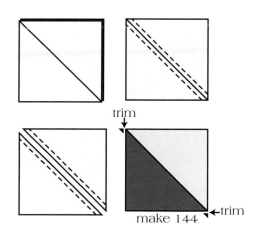

trim

trim

make 144

ASSEMBLING THE GOOSE-IN-THE-POND BLOCKS

1. Arrange 12 half-square triangle units, 4 Rail Fence units, 4 Nine-Patch units, four 3½" light background squares, and one tan 3½" square in configuration for each Goose-in-the-Pond block. Referring to Chain-Piecing Blocks on page 22, sew the units into vertical rows, and press the seam allowance in each row in alternating directions.

2. Referring to Chain-Piecing Blocks on page 22, sew the vertical rows of blocks together, and press the seam allowances in the same direction. Make 12 Goose-in-the-Pond blocks. The Goose-in-the-Pond blocks should measure 15½" square. If necessary, make small adjustments in your seam allowances to make sure your blocks are the correct size.

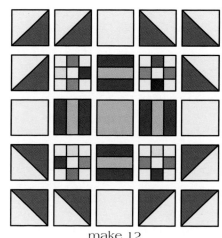

make 12

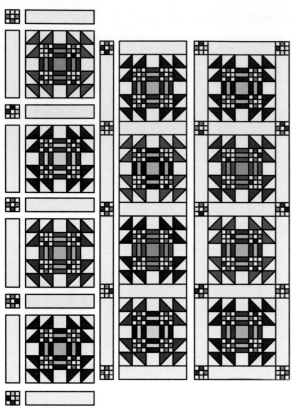

assembling the quilt center

ASSEMBLING THE QUILT CENTER

1. Lay out the 12 Goose-in-the-Pond blocks, 31 sashings and 20 Nine-Patch units in configuration for the quilt center. Referring to Chain-Piecing Blocks on page 22, sew the blocks, sashings, and Nine-Patch units into vertical rows. Press the seam allowances in each vertical row in alternating directions.

2. Referring to the previous diagram, sew the vertical rows together, matching the seam intersections. Press the seam allowances between the vertical rows in the same direction.

ADDING THE PIECED BORDER

1. Mark a diagonal line from corner to corner on forty-four 3⅞" light background squares, referring to Half-Square Triangle Units on page 19.

2. Place the 3⅞" light background squares right sides together with forty-four 3⅞" pink squares, and sew ¼" away from the marked line on both sides. Rotary cut on the marked lines, for a total of 88 half-square triangle units. Press the seam allowances toward the pink fabrics.

3. Sew 12 half-square triangle units, a 3½" light background square, and 12 half-square triangle units together. Make another pieced border like this one, and press the seam allowances away from the 3½" light background center square. Sew these pieced borders to the sides of the quilt center, and press the seam allowances toward the sashing strips.

4. Sew 10 half-square triangle units, a 3½" light background square, and 10 half-square triangle units together. Make another pieced border like this one, and press the seam allowances away from the 3½" light background square. Referring to the quilt diagram, sew these pieced borders to the top and bottom edges of the quilt center.

make 2

make 2

ADDING THE OUTER BORDER

1. Sew three 4½" x 42" light background strips together for each of the two side outer border strips. Sew two 4½" x 42" light background strips for the top and bottom outer border strips. Press the seam allowances open.

2. Measure your quilt top vertically through the center to determine the correct length for the side outer border strips. Cut the longer two light background outer border strips to this measurement, and sew them to the sides of the quilt center. Press the seam allowances toward the outer border strips.

3. Measure your quilt top horizontally through the center to determine the correct length for the top and bottom outer border strips. Cut the shorter two light background outer border strips to this measurement, and sew them to the top and bottom edges of the quilt center, referring to the previous diagram. Press the seam allowances toward the outer border strips.

QUILTING AND FINISHING

1. Press your finished quilt top and mark quilting designs, as desired, referring to Marking Methods on page 30.

2. Prepare the quilt sandwich for quilting, referring to Preparing the Backing on page 29, Layering and Basting on page 31.

3. Quilt by hand or machine, as desired, referring to Hand Quilting on page 31, or Machine Quilting on page 33. I quilted in the ditch of the patchwork seams and chose a curved quilting design to soften the angles of the pieced border.

4. Bind the edges of the quilt and add a hanging sleeve, if desired, referring to Binding on page 33 and Attaching a Hanging Sleeve on page 35.

GOOSE IN THE POND AT DAWN quilt diagram

GOOSE-IN-THE-POND BLOCKS, RAIL FENCE UNITS, AND NINE-PATCH UNITS			
	GOOSE-IN-THE-POND BLOCKS	RAIL FENCE UNITS	NINE-PATCH UNITS
Lap	6	24	36
Full/Queen	20	80	110
King	25	100	136

QUILT SIZES	
Lap	53" x 71"
Full/Queen	89" x 107"
King	107" x 107"

STRIP SETS			
	RAIL FENCE UNITS PINK/TAN/ PINK	NINE-PATCH UNITS LIGHT/PASTEL/ LIGHT	PASTEL/LIGHT/ PASTEL
Lap	3	3	2
Full/Queen	8	8	4
King	10	10	5

FABRICS AND SUPPLIES

	LIGHT BACKGROUND	PINK	PASTEL	TAN
Lap	4 yards	1⅛ yards	½ yard	½ yard
Full/Queen	8⅞ yards	2¼ yards	1¼ yards	¾ yard
King	9½ yards	2¾ yards	1½ yards	1 yard

	BACKING	BATTING
Lap	4 yards	57" x 75"
Full/Queen	9½ yards	93" x 111"
King	9½ yards	111" x 111"

CUTTING LIST

	1½" x 42" LIGHT BACKGROUND STRIPS	3⅞" LIGHT BACKGROUND SQUARES	3½" LIGHT BACKGROUND SQUARES
Lap	8	68	28
Full/Queen	20	176	84
King	25	212	104

	1½" x 42" PINK STRIPS	3⅞" PINK SQUARES	3½" TAN SQUARES
Lap	6	68	6
Full/Queen	16	176	20
King	20	212	25

	1½" x 42" TAN STRIPS	1½" x 42" PASTEL STRIPS
Lap	3	7
Full/Queen	8	16
King	10	20

	3½" x 15½" LIGHT BACKGROUND STRIPS
Lap	17
Full/Queen	49
King	60

	4½" x 42" LIGHT BACKGROUND STRIPS	2⅛" x 42" LIGHT BACKGROUND BINDING STRIPS
Lap	8	6
Full/Queen	12	10
King	12	11

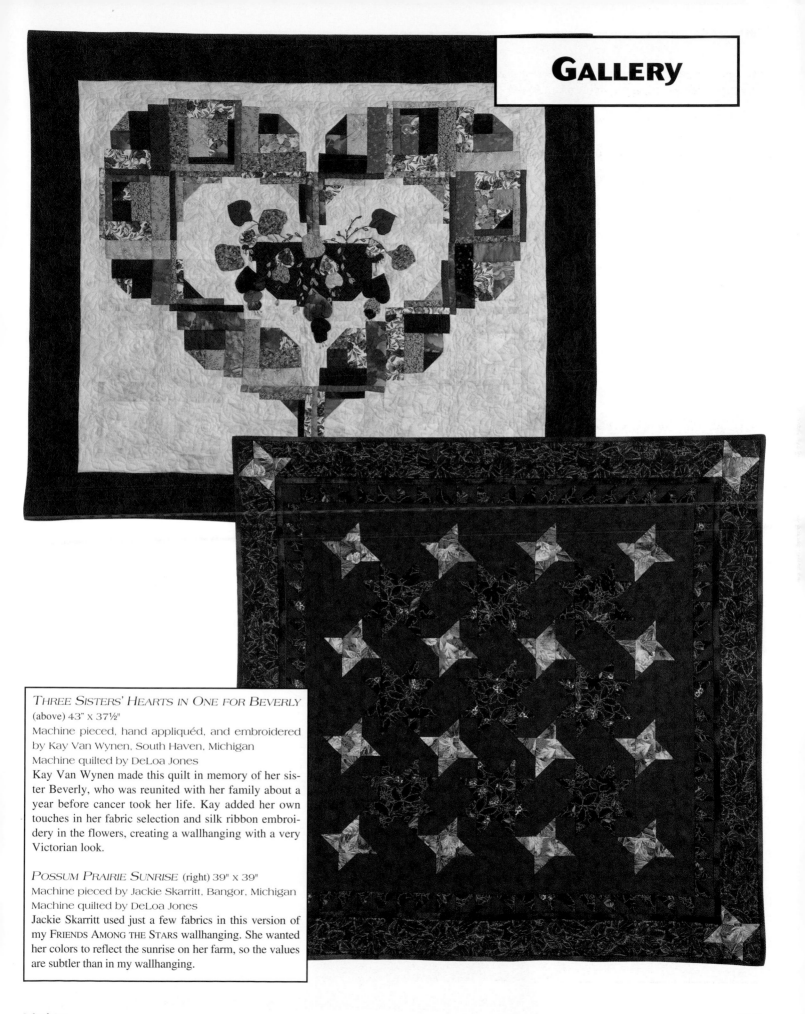

THREE SISTERS' HEARTS IN ONE FOR BEVERLY
(above) 43" x 37½"
Machine pieced, hand appliquéd, and embroidered
by Kay Van Wynen, South Haven, Michigan
Machine quilted by DeLoa Jones
Kay Van Wynen made this quilt in memory of her sister Beverly, who was reunited with her family about a year before cancer took her life. Kay added her own touches in her fabric selection and silk ribbon embroidery in the flowers, creating a wallhanging with a very Victorian look.

POSSUM PRAIRIE SUNRISE (right) 39" x 39"
Machine pieced by Jackie Skarritt, Bangor, Michigan
Machine quilted by DeLoa Jones
Jackie Skarritt used just a few fabrics in this version of my FRIENDS AMONG THE STARS wallhanging. She wanted her colors to reflect the sunrise on her farm, so the values are subtler than in my wallhanging.

*SCRAP QUILTS ACCORDING TO
RUTH* 30" x 37"
Machine pieced by Ruth Tallman,
Coloma, Michigan
Machine quilted by DeLoa Jones
Ruth made this quilt especially for
inclusion in this book! She usually
doesn't make "scrappy" things but
says this one qualifies, because it is
made from fabrics left over from
another project.

EL NIÑO: WIND, WATER, AND MUD
63" x 87"
Machine pieced by Kitty Sorgen, New-
bury Park, California
Hand quilted by Jean Byrd, Middle-
boro, Kentucky, and Debra Duncan,
Tazewell, Tennessee
Kitty made this quilt while I was design-
ing quilts for this book. It matched one of
my sketches so well, we just had to
include it. Kitty's fabric choices give this
quilt an antique quality.

SPRING IN FULL BLOOM (above) 56" x 56"
Machine pieced and quilted by DeLoa Jones
The darker shades of the flower fabrics and the bolder green I
chose for this quilt create a spring-like feel.

WINTER (left) 56" x 56"
Machine pieced by Corinne Wade, Decatur, Michigan
Machine quilted by Deloa Jones
Corinne wanted to complete the seasons quilt series with her
version of winter. The blues and whites are a perfect vision of
white snow against a winter sky on a cold January day.

JENNY'S BLUE GOOSE 78" x 96"
Machine pieced by Sondra Herriman,
Covert, Michigan
Machine quilted by DeLoa Jones
Sondra made this quilt for her grand-
daughter Jenny. She decided on a
palette of scraps in blues against a white
background for a very striking quilt.

SUMMER BLOSSOMS 56" x 56"
Machine pieced by Sandra Moon,
Niles, Michigan
Machine quilted by DeLoa Jones
Sandra chose summer colors instead of
the autumn colors and achieved the look
of summer beautifully with the shading
of both the green and flower fabrics.

BIBLIOGRAPHY

Cory, Pepper, *Mastering Quilt Marking*, C&T Publishing, 1999.

Hargrave, Harriet, *Heirloom Machine Quilting*, C&T Publishing, 1990.

Noble, Maurine, *Machine Quilting Made Easy*, That Patchwork Place, 1994.

RESOURCES

Appliqué flower patterns for THE STARS OF MICHIGAN
Possom Prairie Patterns
c/o DeLoa Jones
15804 M-140
South Haven, MI 49090
616-639-2123
www.deloasquiltshop.com

Acrylic rulers
Marti Michell
P.O. Box 802118
Atlanta, GA 30366
770-458-6500
cservice@frommarti.com

Finger wraps
Wrap It Thimble
Quilter's Rule Int'l. LLC
817 Mohr Ave
Waterford, WI 53185
1-800-343-8671
www.quiltersrule.com

Appliqué and quilting needles
Glue baste
Roxanne Products Co.
742 Granite Ave.
Lathrop, CA 95330
www.thatperfectstitch.com
1-800-993-4445

Rotating rotary cutting mats
Brooklyn Revolver mat
Come Quilt With Me
39003 Avenue I
Brooklyn, NY 11210
http://www.quiltfest.com/wfw/wfw00/yamin.htm

ABOUT THE AUTHOR

DeLoa Jones has been a quilter since 1979 and started teaching quiltmaking classes in 1983. She has taught in several shops in several states and has won many awards in local quilt shows. One of her quilts was selected for the Houston International quilt show in 1991. DeLoa has made commissioned hand-done quilts and wallhangings and started her own machine quilting business in South Haven, Michigan, where she lives with her husband and eight children. She continues to teach quiltmaking workshops and lecture in shops and guilds throughout the country.

JUST PEACHY 86" x 106"
Machine pieced and hand quilted by Barbara Grogan, Benton Harbor, Michigan
Barbara used brown and green to reflect life on the farm and chose peach to express the feminine element of this Farmer's Daughter pattern. She also changed the values in the border blocks, which gives the border a whole new look.

OTHER AQS BOOKS

This is only a small selection of the books available from the American Quilter's Society. AQS books are known worldwide for timely topics, clear writing, beautiful color photos, and accurate illustrations and patterns. The following books are available from your local bookseller, quilt shop, or public library.

#6076   US$21.95

#5759   US$19.95

#6009   US$19.95

#6073   US$19.95

#6005   US$19.95

#5710   US$19.95

#6036   US$24.95

#5848   US$19.95

#6079   US$21.95